Praise

"Hennelly brilliantly analyzes our capitalist crises and how individuals cope with them, tragically but often heroically. He helps us draw inspiration and realistic hope from how courageous Americans are facing and fixing a stuck nation."

Richard D. Wolff, Economist and author of *The Sickness is the System: When Capitalism Fails to Save Us from Pandemics or Itself*

"With the skill of a seasoned reporter drawing from an impressive trove of scholarship and first-hand experience, Hennelly artfully presents a granular narrative of the political economy of contemporary US society that is simultaneously enlightening, infuriating and inspirational. Stuck Nation reads like a kind of updating and reframing of the modern contradictions of capitalism on a timeline that includes presidents Obama, Trump, Biden, the COVID-19 pandemic and the rise of the Amazon gig economy. Echoing Howard Zinn's classic People's History of the United States, Stuck Nation is a must read for those interested in extending democracy and combating racism, especially trade unionists, educators and social activists seeking justice, equality, and a new world order— from the bottom up!"

Joe Wilson, PhD, Labor historian & Political Scientist

"One of journalism's prized possessions, investigative reporter Bob Hennelly has occupied a relentless forward position on every major issue of our time: from housing to healthcare, from education, economics, and social justice, to voting rights and labor. A specialist in drilling down into the core of where real people live and work, Hennelly gathers his materials on the ground, to unleash the toughest, most uncomfortable questions on those at the top of the ivory tower power chain. While much of our contempora protects the status quo, Hennelly can be found rummagin; the back alleys and ravaged, foreclosed-on, job and food neighborhoods of Newark and New York City, using his own reporting as the brick and mortar to ram the complacent underpinnings of the country on behalf of working-class people. To those like myself who have long depended on his pieces, *Stuck Nation* gathers the marrow of Hennelly's work into one sustained, impassioned, and always detail-oriented argument, and serves as a primer for those who will no doubt find themselves returning often for more from the workshop of a master."

Max Pizarro, Insider NJ executive editor

"Finally! Veteran investigative journalist Hennelly helps us understand the economic counterrevolution that set the stage for the NeoAuthoritarian Right — including Trump's rise and the January 6th near-putsch in DC. He precisely describes how unaccountable global capital has managed to capture country after country, systematically avoiding taxation and regulation while shifting the costs of essential social services to working families, small business, and the poor. One predictable effect is the collapse of public health and civil service, foreshadowing the outrageous mishandling of the pandemic in countries like the US, the UK, India, Brazil, Italy, and Russia that have the world's strongest neo-authoritarian movements. Another dire consequence is the stalled effort to address the global climate crisis as well as soaring inequality — even while untaxed and heavily subsidized billionaires soar into space. Fortunately, Hennelly provides some reasons to hope - he shows how all across the US, community groups and labor activists are reviving the combination of practical organizing plus a truly progressive agenda that is essential to get our 'Stuck Nation' — and our 'stuck planet' — unstuck. A must read."

James S. Henry, Esq., Investigative journalist, economist and lawyer. Global Justice Fellow, Yale University.

Stuck Nation:

Can the United States Change Course on Our History of Choosing Profits Over People?

By

Robert Hennelly

Other Books from Democracy at Work:

The Sickness is the System: When Capitalism Fails to Save Us from Pandemics or Itself by Richard D. Wolff

Understanding Socialism by Richard D. Wolff

Understanding Marxism by Richard D. Wolff

To my loving wife Debbie
and change agents everywhere

Table of Contents

Foreword by Richard D. Wolff

The feeling of being stuck in a situation you do not want to be in happens at times in everyone's life. It becomes an historic moment when huge portions of a nation feel that way. Sure, people point to different causes and reasons for a stuck nation. Yet the fact that so many people feel that way at the same time is profoundly significant. And this remarkable book by Bob Hennelly succeeds in proving exactly that.

Critics, victims, and mere observers of US capitalism have been deeply shaken over recent years. Instability has become frightening with three crashes in the first 20 years of this century: dot-com in 2000, subprime mortgage in 2008, and COVID-19 in 2020. Each was worse than the one before. Their chosen names suggest the crashes were caused by events external or exceptional to the capitalist economic system's normalcy. But the truth is that capitalism has always and everywhere suffered periodic crashes (the "business cycle") on average every four to seven years. So this century's US capitalist crashes are right on schedule. The nation seems stuck in worsening instability.

US capitalism's inequality has become socially divisive to the point of explosion. Even when unified by everyone's vulnerability to a viral pandemic, an unequal nation responded unequally. Middle-income people and the poor suffered far more than the rich. A nation with four percent of the world's population suffered 20 percent of COVID deaths through mid-2021. So deeply has inequality worked its way into US society that even a shared public health crisis only made it more extreme. We seem to be a nation stuck in worsening inequality.

3

The same politicians in both major parties regularly bemoan the instability and the inequality. They deny that those problems are systemic qualities. Therefore, they insist that no systemic change is needed to solve them. The result is that we seem systemically stuck with them. Since they are worsening, so too is our stuckness. Political discourse and overlapping regional differences sharpen. Old scapegoats are revived to serve again as targets for rebellion against feeling stuck. Opportunism beckons aspiring politicians and entrepreneurs – likewise overlapping categories – to advance careers and make profits by pandering to every misbegotten effort to escape stuckness. At all costs – and they are many – mainstream media, politicians, and academics work to keep system change off the public agenda.

Bob Hennelly is a superb investigative reporter with decades of journalistic experience in print, radio, and TV. He expertly connects the macroeconomics of capitalist crises and the microlevel immediate personal lives of those navigating those crises. Readers get to see the system from both perspectives and thereby achieve levels of understanding more adequate to the crisis we are all living through. He chronicles the heroes, victims, and the mixtures of both in our fellow Americans. We recognize them but see and appreciate them anew in his writing. Compassion, wit, and a knowing skepticism inform his interviews. He captures not only how his interviewees wrestle with the key decisions they must make, but also the social and personal costs of their thoughts and actions.

We live in "interesting times," an unprecedented coincidence in time and space of a global capitalist crash and a deadly global pandemic. It is hard to grasp these times, to process them in ways that can make us and our relationships stronger. To do that, we need books like this that enable us to learn from others making the same effort. Bob Hennelly's book helps us to become unstuck, personally and politically, to free ourselves from a declining capitalism. It is animated throughout by the theme that we can do better.

Stuck Nation also speaks directly and instructively to activists. Successful organizing for social change requires that activists know their audiences intimately and know what urgencies impose upon them now. Those audiences have specific ideas about what changes

4

are possible, what social alliances and coalitions might be built and what paths followed to make the targeted social changes. This book respectfully (yet also constructively and critically) explores the labor movement, organized and unorganized, to see how its actuality and potentialities might open further the space for social transition beyond a stuck capitalism.

In the best and most productive sense of the term, *Stuck Nation* is a "book for our times." We at DemocracyatWork.info are proud and excited to be publishing it.

Prologue

I selected "@stucknation" as my Twitter handle shortly before I left WNYC-New York Public Radio in 2013, where I had been covering New Jersey and New York City for several years. By that time, I had spent more than 20 years covering local, state, and national politics — long enough to see a discernible pattern of American stagnation where, regardless of the issue, the forces of capital prevailed over labor. No matter what injustice would catch fire, politicians would gain traction by appearing to address it just long enough to win elections; yet, the underlying problem that had sparked public protest was left to fester. From gun violence to local flooding from over-development, public calls for reform would crest and dissipate as the commercial forces that profited from the status quo endured.

When President Obama was just into his second term, I could see that in places where I was reporting — like Newark and Paterson, New Jersey — things had actually continued to deteriorate from the Great Recession. There was a disturbing disconnect between the MSNBC, NPR, *New York Times* rhetoric of recovery and my lived and reported experience. At street level, in the neighborhoods in which I had reported before Obama was elected, the slide had continued. The same mortgage predators just paid their Department of Justice fines but continued their corrupt practices, driving primarily African American families from their homes that had been in families for generations, leaving a devastated streetscape of zombie homes and disrepair.

The property values in these neighborhoods, which had already been redlined by longstanding, race-based mortgage discrimination, just continued to decline. How did these local governments, invariably presided over by Democratic machines, respond? By raising the property taxes on the dwindling number of households that somehow were still holding on. African Americans got bragging rights for having a Black man in the White House, but millions of them lost their own homes. This was just more evidence of a "Stuck Nation"— so stuck because its leadership was cut off and willfully blind to the circumstances of a broad swath of the country, particularly people of color.

In my WNYC interview with then-Senator Obama on March 27, 2008, he had a serious command of the national economy and the global situation. He also possessed a self-effacing sense of humor. I was impressed with him. He said that WNYC was a great radio station; and I said the pay was okay too, considering it was public radio, but added that I was married to a lawyer. He said, "That was my plan too," and smiled.

He was in the city prior to the New York Democratic primary, and I rode with him and Robert Gibbs in his black SUV, along with his Secret Service detail, between his speaking engagements. By coincidence, my wife Debbie and I had recently attended her friend's wedding in Chicago, which was officiated by Reverend Jeremiah Wright, the Obamas' controversial pastor. Wright's frank comments about how the US's militaristic foreign policy had set the stage for 9/11 were all over the New York tabloids at the time. We spoke briefly about that, and I told Obama I was actually a Deacon in the United Church of Christ, the same liberal Christian denomination in which Wright was a minister. His relief was apparent. Looking back at it, the interview was quite timely, allowing him to change the narrative from the persistent focus on his connection to Reverend Wright.

The New York Times took note of the interview, zeroing in on Obama's endorsement of then-Mayor Michael Bloomberg's controversial congestion-pricing plan, which aimed to reduce pollution from vehicles and fund mass transit. Ironically, we were stuck in typical Manhattan traffic, traveling from Cooper Union in Lower Manhattan to a hotel in Midtown. Obama's answers to my questions, spanning from the perils of offshore banking to foreign policy, were

8

smooth and considered. But his vague response on the question of the essential need for a shift in the US's policy on drugs — away from a criminal justice approach to a public health focus — made me realize that he was more of a charismatic moderate than a change agent.

Inside the WNYC newsroom, my assessment that he could actually beat Hillary Clinton was an outlier. Traveling through Texas during the primary season, I saw how nimble the Obama campaign was and how they had empowered ground-level campaign volunteers; while the Clinton campaign was an old-school, top-down, command-and-control operation.

On August 28, 2008, I was in Denver's Mile High Stadium when Obama accepted his party's nomination as its presidential candidate. I was standing with Reverend Al Sharpton and Reverend Jesse Jackson, on whose 1984 presidential campaign I had worked, as the sense of limitless possibilities surged through the capacity crowd. "Four years ago, I stood before you and told you my story, of the brief union between a young man from Kenya and a young woman from Kansas, who weren't well-off or well-known, but shared a belief that in America their son could achieve whatever he put his mind to," Obama told the adoring crowd.

On the night of the 2008 general election, I decided the best place from which to file my reporting throughout the night would be the Rutgers New Brunswick campus. It was a place where the college students really had to fight hard to get to vote, because the local election authorities saw them as interlopers. When the networks called the election for Obama, the wave of youthful exuberance surging out of those dormitory buildings and into New Brunswick's night air was electric, as college students even embraced police officers who were swarmed by a tsunami of joy.

Just three years later, in September 2011, I would be covering the Occupy Wall Street Movement, which had taken root in its prolonged encampment in lower Manhattan's Zuccotti Park. I recorded hours of interviews with the primarily young activists who had come from all over the nation to camp out in the canyons of Wall Street and protest an economy that was increasingly rigged against them. No doubt, they had been Obama voters. For them, hope and change had become despair and stagnation. Many were buried under mountains of debt for college educations that society had told them they needed as the foundation for a good life. But for so many, that turned out to be a dead-end of living in their parents' basements.

The global war on terror was now over a decade long, and Uncle Sam just seemed to be a robot stuck spinning his wheels in a deepening rut on foreign soil. In 2004, I had covered a pancake breakfast at the Westwood, New Jersey, National Guard Armory, where the wives, families, and friends of troops deployed in Iraq were raising money at $6-a-plate to help keep the utilities on and the mortgage paid on the homes of these patriots fighting this further-notice war.

"Stuck Nation" seemed completely apropos on so many levels.

This stuck-ness was even manifest in the way New Jersey would flood in the same places year after year, where the bipartisan complicity in real estate development had permitted filling in wetlands, blowing up mountains, and clearing forests; only to be "surprised" when, year after year, people's basements flooded.

In October 2012, I was out and about gathering the news for WNYC in Morris County, New Jersey, when Hurricane Sandy hit with devastating winds and driving rains that were like nothing I had ever experienced. I was inside the Mendham Township emergency headquarters when the dispatcher got the report of the first storm-related deaths in the state, a married couple whose vehicle was crushed by a falling tree when they had gone out to check on their horses.

Early the next day, Governor Christie's press office asked me to be one of two pool reporters in a National Guard helicopter, documenting the Governor's assessment of the impacts of Hurricane Sandy on Sayreville, a working-class community on the banks of the Raritan Bay, where rapacious over-development had caused chronic flooding for years. In the minutes before we landed, I could see from the air how an eight-foot storm surge from the Atlantic Ocean through the Raritan Bay had moved scores of small and modest homes off of their cinder-block foundations. When we landed, I heard the sound of dozens of women weeping, evoking the kind of misery in the landscape that reporters encounter after an earthquake or a missile attack in a residential neighborhood.

For the weeks, months, and years after Sandy, I tracked how working-class neighborhoods, like the one I visited that day, struggled to recover. Many of the homeowners who found themselves under water during Sandy were also under water financially, because the Obama administration had failed to effectively combat the mortgage industry's predatory practices that had caused the Great Collapse in 2008.

As the Obama years drew to a close, the Economic Policy Institute (EPI) observed astutely that the country had "suffered from rising income inequality and chronically slow growth in the living standards of low- and moderate-income Americans." The 2015 EPI analysis continued, "This disappointing living-standards growth — which was in fact caused by rising income inequality — preceded the Great Recession and continues to this day. Fortunately, income inequality and middle-class living standards are now squarely on the political agenda. But despite their increasing salience, these issues are too often discussed in abstract terms. Ignored is the easy-to-understand root of rising income inequality, slow living-standards growth, and a host of other key economic challenges: the near stagnation of hourly wage growth for the vast majority of American workers over the past generation. Countering that by generating broad-based wage growth is our core economic policy challenge."

By Labor Day 2016, after eight years of Obama, America's workers were really stuck and even losing ground, as wealth concentration and income disparity actually accelerated. Despite adding 10 million jobs over his tenure, 1.6 million working-age Americans actually dropped out of the workforce. The labor force participation rate slid from 66 percent to a low of 62.6 percent under Obama.

The erosion of the middle class that has been in the making at least since the 1970s — when American workers stopped seeing their wages grow at a pace with their increasing productivity — was continuing. By August 2016, EPI reported that from 1973 until 2015, while productivity was increasing more than 73 percent, hourly pay for workers went up only 11 percent. In other words, productivity grew by more than six times the rise in wages earned by workers.

11

For decades, American workers had been losing their leverage, as the world's biggest corporations were able to successfully play one country's workforce off another. But now the same corporate interests, which had sparked the race to the bottom for wages and worker benefits between countries, were increasingly turning to robots and automation to reduce their human workforce planet-wide. In 2016, the BBC reported Foxconn, the Chinese-based manufacturer that is the key supplier for Apple and Samsung, cut its workforce by more than half — down to just 50,000 — with the introduction of robots.[1] "Economists have issued dire warnings about how automation will affect the job market, with one report from Deloitte, in partnership with Oxford University, suggesting that 35 percent of jobs will be at risk over the next 20 years," reported the BBC.[2]

"I was at the National Restaurant Show yesterday, and if you look at the robotic devices that are coming into the restaurant industry — it's cheaper to buy a $35,000 robotic arm[3] than it is to hire an employee who is inefficient making $15 an hour bagging French fries — it's nonsense, and it's very destructive, and it's inflationary, and it's going to cause a job loss across this country like you're not going to believe," former McDonald's USA CEO Ed Rensi told FOX Business in an interview.

Jobs with healthcare benefits were increasingly hard to find as corporations, like Uber, figured out how to profit from the increasing precarity of the workforce. The rideshare-app company benefited considerably from the counsel of former Obama campaign manager David Plouffe, who became Uber's policy chief in 2014, as it bullied its way into local markets and destroyed the existing local cab business model along the way.

By 2016, after eight years of struggle, packaged as recovery, millions of voters were ripe for Trump's picking. A critical number of Obama voters of color just stayed home, and Clinton was not perceived as a change agent.

From the oligarchs' point of view, there was nothing better than Trump's strategy of having the victims of predatory, multinational capitalism all go after each other over issues like race and national origin. What you don't want is a peaceful convergence of left and right; better to have everybody fractionalized and alienated, scrambling for a share of the scraps. Both of the major parties had long been co-opted at the top by these corporate interests, puppet masters pulling strings behind the scenes to become the Treasury Secretary or appointed to desirable ambassadorships. It was all pay-to-play, no matter who the players were.

In the 2016 primary on the Democratic side, the presence of the superdelegates insulated former Secretary of State Hillary Clinton a bit from the vagaries of the ballot box. As skillfully as Senator Bernie Sanders executed his insurgent campaign, he still had to continue to try to offer praise for President Obama, whose two terms saw America's income and wealth disparities only widen, with middle-income and poor Americans continuing to lose ground. The big banks had only gotten bigger, the war on terror had widened, and the clamp-down on government whistleblowers had only escalated.

By the South Carolina Republican primary, a state where active-duty and retired military are a big part of the Republican base, it became clear that the Republican National Committee (RNC) had lost its troops, as Donald Trump won the state's 50 delegates, despite having called out President George W. Bush for waging an unnecessary war on Iraq under false pretenses. The bipartisan overuse and abuse of America's volunteer military had left many of these patriotic families fractured by suicide, addiction, long-term disability and divorce. They, like the residents of Iraq and Afghanistan, knew the real price of these unending conflicts.

When both Trump and Sanders carried Michigan, it became clear that the rising anger within the electorate was about an America that no longer worked for American workers. What we had on our hands was a political predator class that had been ignoring the social and economic circumstances of the vast majority of people for a long time and had profited by doing so. They kept themselves in power by serving the richest of the rich, cynically playing regions of the country and segments of the population against one another.

American multinationals avoided paying hundreds of billions of dollars in taxes every year, transferring the tax burden to small business and working people. We were misled to suspect the undocumented among us are the real drag on our national treasury.

13

Yet these folks, one in three of whom own homes here in the US, pay billions of dollars in taxes each year.[4] Likewise, when unions were chased out of the private sector but made inroads in the public sector, big money interests proceeded to demonize public unions for getting the type of pay and benefits that the rest of us were denied, because (they alleged) the new global trade imperative would not permit it.

We were all supposed to become lean-and-mean, like a vast team of Borax mules, pulling the billionaires' dreams of global domination over the finish line. And for this great favor and opportunity — to work for ever-shrinking wages, higher taxes, and less security — we are supposed to deify the billionaires as paragons of philanthropy, elevated on golden media thrones of their own design.

Now, it seemed, it was time to smash some idols.

Sanders's and Trump's Michigan moments were about a working-class America chained, headed up a downward escalator. Unable to ascend those stairs no matter how many hours we would work, or how many coupons we would clip. And sad to say, our kids, who went to college just like we demanded, were chained a few treads below us, by their own debt, as we all trudged in place on that same grand escalator to nowhere. As the 2016 Department of Labor data indicated, the average workweek was shrinking down to 34.5 hours a week, which is below full-time. Wages were down as well. Welcome to part-time America.

For me, then 60 years old, this was no abstraction. My three 20-something daughters were all college-educated, working and living independently, but had massive amounts of college debt that we were (and still are) all trying to pay off. I had been working as a reporter and broadcaster for decades. Over the years, the deflation in writers' fees had been dramatic. Stories that used to garner $1 a word now got a fraction of that. The goal-line stance of almost every going concern in media was to avoid actually employing anyone, so you were reduced to the realm of the so-called "independent contractor," yet always happy to have the work.

Despite working with several different outlets, I had to start working overnight at the local supermarket on the night crew — for $9.13 an hour. The three other guys I worked with were a bit younger than I

14

and were paid more than twice what I was getting, because they were legacy union employees. They represented several decades of experience stocking shelves overnight, checking freshness dates, and really caring about what they put on the shelves for people they rarely saw.

I remember thinking how great a piece of time-lapse video it would have made to see how 1,000 cartons on 10 pallets, 10 feet high, get broken down, spotted on the aisles, and put on the shelves. It wasn't all that pretty. I have to admit to stumbling a bit trying to move those massive bags of dog food at 3 a.m. off of a pallet that had been packed at the central warehouse by a robot. It was like trying to toss a waterbed alone or steer a really drunk dance partner to a graceful ending. And who would have known the vast choices available for kitty litter? That was 21st-century America: infinite choices for all the shit that doesn't really matter.

It was a union shop, and my co-workers made a decent wage, had healthcare insurance, and weeks of paid vacation. I had none of that, and my big consolation prize was outperforming the 29-year-old who started the same week I did, whom they subsequently let go. I didn't begrudge my union mates the wage and benefits they earned over a lifetime of service. I just wanted to know why the union to which I paid dues seemed to stop trying for the new hires. I had been writing about income inequality for years, but it really didn't hit me until that first paycheck, when I had worked 35 hours and saw that my take-home pay was only $270. I was handling cans of olive oil that cost twice my hourly wage.

I had tried to stay in shape, but after a few weeks of moving around massive quantities of bottled water, flour, and sugar, I realized I was using muscles I hadn't used for decades. Ironically, their last use was in my young adulthood, when I worked at a Shop-Rite in Ramsey, New Jersey, also stocking shelves and also in a union shop. Back then, I was making enough money, above the minimum wage, to live on my own and pay my tuition — then, less than $400 per semester — to go to Ramapo College, a state school. Factoring in inflation, I was making more money in the late '70s than I was in the 21st century.

I was eventually able to quit the night crew after receiving a sizable grant to do a series of investigative reports for WBGO-Newark Public

Radio, exploring the real-life stories of struggle that had been missed even in the relatively progressive editorial atmosphere of public radio.

Affordable housing has been at the nexus of so much of the dislocation on which I have been reporting for decades — now more than 40 years after the New Jersey Supreme Court's landmark Mount Laurel decision was hailed nationally for proclaiming it was unconstitutional for local zoning to exclude housing for its poor and working class.[5] Decades later, New Jersey was still in a full-blown affordable-housing crisis[6] and was leading the nation in foreclosures.[7] And despite the scarcity of affordable housing, there were tens of thousands of vacant homes just wasting away.

How stuck was this nation?!

In January 2015, Kevin Walsh — an attorney with the advocacy group Fair Share Housing — was before New Jersey's highest court making the case it was time for the courts to step back in, because their Mount Laurel decision had been ignored. He described how Governor Christie had hollowed out the Council on Affordable Housing, which was created by the legislature to implement the court's landmark 1975 ruling. "It's 15 years in which the rights that Mount Laurel recognized have gone unenforced with real human consequences, so we come to the court and say please do what you promised to do," Kevin Walsh told the justices.[8]

In 2018, I told a too-common story of the lack of affordable housing, through the lived experience of a pair of 20-somethings living in their car. Kelee Patterson and her boyfriend Tim Johnson know all too well about the failure to live up to Mount Laurel's 43-year-old mandate. They spent the winter of 2018 living in Patterson's car with her three dogs. Almost six years after Super Storm Sandy had hit this part of Monmouth County, along the Route 35 corridor, finding affordable housing is impossible.

"In the front seat, we put the little dog on the floor on where I drive," Patterson explained. "The driver seat has two little dogs. On the seat there is one dog, and on the floor, there is one little dog. Then the big dog is on the passenger seat with the seat laid down. Then we cuddle up in the back. We make that in with blankets and pillows. All our clothes are in the back."

Patterson tried to remain positive about the couple's prospects and a pending job interview later that day. "I would love to be in my own home to wake up and brush my teeth, shower and go to work... because right now we go to Target, Quick-Check bathrooms to get ready for an interview, and thank God we have an interview." "I hope we get these jobs. Get these jobs and save money and get to a state where the cost of living isn't so high and move there," Johnson added.

Inside MJ's Pizza in Middletown over a late lunch, Patterson and Johnson explained how it came to be that two college graduates in their 20s ended up homeless and battling addiction issues. Patterson recounted the story of her mother's home in Middletown that the family lost in foreclosure.[9] "My mom has lived there for 18 years, and so have I," she said. "I went to college twice and got two degrees: nursing and health science. Got my two degrees; came home. I moved out on my own several times, but I always came back to Mom's, when the relationship did not work out or the drug addiction got too bad, and I could not pay my rent. My mom is a single mom and been a hard worker her whole life."

For Johnson, his life was upended when his father came down with pancreatic cancer and in just a few months died. His mother fell behind on the mortgage payments. "I had a similar story with foreclosure too; my mother was foreclosed in 2002," he said. "When my father passed away, our house was foreclosed. She had to sell it before it was foreclosed."

Johnson's mom's home in Middletown was still listed as vacant when I finished reporting the story (in 2018). It was one of nearly 40,000 empty homes throughout New Jersey at the time.

In this book, I share my observations on the origins of our national stuck-ness, my reporting on how it endures, and my analysis of what might be required for us to change the course of our historical patterns. I've written this book while our country has been in the convulsions of a global pandemic that had been long predicted by public health experts. Yet the nation and the planet were caught so unprepared that millions would die; and, as of this writing, 115,000 healthcare workers around the world have perished.

And in the midst of this once-in-a-century public health crisis, the United States itself — despite the expenditure of trillions of dollars in military procurement and global deployment in the name of protecting democracy — was almost toppled from within by one of the two national political parties that had been commandeered by a white-supremacist authoritarian.

In the pages ahead, you will read accounts of individuals and a broader movement willing to put everything at risk to change our national narrative, so that America can begin what Reverend Dr. William Barber and the Poor People's Campaign have described as a "Third Reconstruction" — putting the condition of the people ahead of profits.

Chapter 1: Contradictions of the American Brand

On January 18, 2021 — Martin Luther King Day — we were processing two of the contradictory narratives in our "American Experiment," born of our enduring ambivalence about race and equality that has haunted and defined our nation from its inception. Our global brand may be equality, but the lived experience of tens of millions of Americans is one of stark inequality.

Even as 245 years have passed since the signing of our Declaration of Independence, we remain very much a "Stuck Nation." It should really come as no surprise.

Our nation came into existence through its complicity in two crimes against humanity: (1) the enslavement of African people; and (2) the ethnic cleansing of the Native inhabitants encountered here by white European settlers, who claimed dominion over all they saw when they landed on behalf of a God no one could see. Scroll forward to January 20, 2021, when President-elect Joe Biden and Senator Kamala Harris were sworn in as president and vice president, marking the unprecedented elevation of a woman, who is also a person of color, to the second-highest office of the land. Progress? This absolutely was a step forward in validating our stated ideals of racial and gender equality.

Yet tens of thousands of armed members of the National Guard stood in the foreground of this historic tableau. They were deployed to fend off a potential attack by aggrieved Trump supporters and white supremacists who had violently stormed our Capitol just two weeks earlier, and many had threatened to return.

That January 6th attack resulted in the suspension of Congress's certification of the results of the Electoral College vote for several hours, the murder of Capitol Police Officer Brian Sicknick, and the brutal beating of dozens of other police officers. In one of the many disturbing images that day, an insurrectionist paraded the battle flag of the Confederacy inside our Capitol — something that had never been allowed to happen before in American history, not even during the Civil War.

Fifty-seven years ago, Norman Rockwell created the iconic painting "The Problem We All Live With" depicting Ruby Bridges, a six-year-old African American girl being escorted into a racially segregated New Orleans elementary school by US Marshalls. Rockwell's iconic painting recently enjoyed a new life as a meme on social media due to Senator Harris's own history as a child of color who was bused to school in order to break the white color barrier. On Inauguration Day, Senator Harris was sworn in by Supreme Court Justice Sonia Sotomayor — the first woman of color to join our country's highest court — under the watchful eye of tens of thousands of members of the National Guard and a small army of local, state, and federal law enforcement.

Meanwhile, across the country, a once-in-a-century public health crisis — which hits the poor and people of color the hardest — continues to grip the nation in the absence of a nationally coordinated plan in place to eradicate it. By January 2021, the COVID-19 pandemic was killing more Americans in a single day than were killed on the day of the September 11th attack.

Is this what progress looks like in America's federalist democracy, almost halfway through its third century of existence?

After the attempted coup on January 6, 2021, FBI court filings and news reports revealed the central role of active-duty and retired members of law enforcement and the military in the violent attack on our Capitol.[10] Several news outlets, including *The New York Times*, reported instances in which individual Capitol Police were videotaped that day opening up the barricades to the seething mob and even posing for selfies with the rioters.[11] On January 12, *USA Today* reported that two Capitol Police officers were suspended and ten more were under investigation.

General Russel Honore, who was subsequently tapped by House Speaker Nancy Pelosi to investigate the attack, told MSNBC he was "surprised the Pentagon did not have the National Guard on standby" that day and that there was a "major failure in intelligence" by the FBI.[12] Moreover, Honore, who rose to prominence by virtue of his leadership during Hurricane Katrina, raised the possibility that the lack of internal preparations for the long-planned mass event suggested there could have been "complicity" at the highest levels of the on-scene command structure.

It would not be until the end of January that the public would learn just how brutally violent the Trump insurrectionists' attack had been and just how fierce was the hand-to-hand combat the Capitol Police had to engage in to regain control of the Capitol. Close to 140 Capitol Police and Washington, D.C., police officers were injured with dozens more testing positive for COVID-19. "I've talked to officers who have done two tours in Iraq who said this was scarier to them than their time in combat," said acting Washington, D.C., Police Chief Robert Contee III, according to *The Washington Post*.

In just a matter of a few weeks the FBI had identified close to two dozen active-duty police officers and active military who were allegedly in the ranks of the insurrectionists. On January 28, the Pentagon confirmed that in 2020 the FBI had opened up 143 investigations into active-duty and retired military —"68 of those for domestic extremism," according to the *Military Times*. On February 3, newly-sworn-in Defense Secretary Lloyd Austin would order a 60-day stand-down across all of the US Armed Forces for the purpose of an internal review of the prevalence of extremism in the active-duty ranks of the US military.

The possibility of law enforcement complicity in the January 6th riot would not come as a surprise to 83-year-old Paul McLemore. In 1961 McLemore became the first African American to join the ranks of the New Jersey State Police, which is celebrating its 100th anniversary in

2021. McLemore remained a New Jersey State Trooper until 1976, and he went on to become a civil-rights attorney and municipal court judge. "No question about it — there is no way that could have happened without the active participation and cooperation of law enforcement; and I say that based on experience in law enforcement, having been in the Marines, and being on the bench," McLemore said. "I draw on all of those experiences."

The retired judge said that historically racist sentiments and actions by the police have long been tolerated internally and rarely were seen within the command structure as being equivalent with lawlessness or other forms of enterprise corruption. "I have seen evidence of that, no question," McLemore said. "In addition to the morbid brutality that's been imposed on African American communities in our cities by police officers, they have committed crimes against the same population — stealing money from them, planting evidence on them. I know that happens."

I first interviewed McLemore more than 20 years ago, when I was writing for *New Jersey Monthly*, researching the allegations by a New Jersey State Police trooper of color, Sgt. Vincent Belleran, who had blown the whistle on the systemic use of racial profiling within the elite unit. Belleran was punished for bringing attention to the unconstitutional practice, which ultimately the state had to promise to end under a 1999 consent decree with the Department of Justice, after decades of enabling the illegal behavior.

It's important to keep in mind what was happening during the 1960s when McLemore joined the NJ State Police. Dr. Martin Luther King's Civil-Rights message, which embraced anti-war and pro-labor themes, was considered a threat to national security by then-FBI Director Jay Edgar Hoover — who, with his covert operation "COINTELPRO" (abbreviated from COunter INTELligence PROgram), illegally tried to subvert and discredit King and his movement.

In the 1950s, McLemore, who was at the top of his high school class in Buffalo, New York, had wanted to become a physician but was steered by his guidance counselor to go into the military instead. When high school graduation came and he missed out on winning the scholarships his classmates were garnering, McLemore took his

22

guidance counselor's advice. "I was in Marine boot camp on Parris Island when I found out I'd got five scholarships," McLemore recalled. "That was my fault with my impetuosity. If I had been just a little bit patient, my whole life could have been different. But I don't regret how things went down, because I would not be the man I am now." McLemore stayed on the New Jersey State Troopers until 1976, when he left to pursue his legal career.

In the summer of 1967, during Newark's civil unrest, McLemore was an African American NJ State Police trooper on the ground in the "Brick City." Our paths crossed in the 1990s, when I was writing about racial profiling in the NJ State Police, and I cold-called McLemore to see if he would be willing to discuss the internal culture of the NJ State Police. He put me off with a sort of homework assignment: I would get my interview, but first I would have to find and read something called the *Lilley Report*, which had been issued by a panel convened in August of 1967 by Gov. Richard Hughes to investigate the circumstances surrounding the several days of unrest in Newark in July1967, which left 26 dead and more than 700 injured.

I went to the local Morris County Library and located the report of *The Governor's Select Commission on Civil Disorder* (also known as the *Lilley Report*, after its chairman, then AT&T President Robert D. Lilley).[13] I spent hours with it, because what it described was — as Newark civil-rights activist Junius W. Williams told *The New York Times* in 2017 — actually a "police riot."[14]

Racial tensions had been simmering in Newark for months before July 1967, when the brutal police beating of a Black cab driver, who had been pulled over for a traffic violation, caused things to boil over. The national Civil Rights Movement was gaining momentum, and the city's Black community was becoming more assertive. Heavy-handed land-use decisions by the white municipal power structure, such as the decision to locate a new medical school in the heart of the Black community, displacing longtime residents, generated organized pushback. African Americans felt they were being taken for granted by the white politicians they had supported for generations but were systematically cut out of city contracts that went to the white power structure's patrons.

23

Over the next 24 hours, the Newark Police Department tried to keep a lid on a very dynamic situation. Cab drivers were mobilized to protest the treatment of their colleague, community members were protesting police brutality, and street conditions were deteriorating. Police were being pelted with debris, and looting was breaking out.

McLemore was ordered to report to the NJ State Police barracks at Hightstown in his riot gear. According to media accounts, fires were burning out of control in Newark's central city. He joined a caravan of state police cars with hundreds of troopers heading up the New Jersey Turnpike, lights flashing. "The guys with me were just ecstatic, like they were going off to war," McLemore said of the white troopers with whom he rode. "We got to where the Newark airport is. You could see Newark's skyline and all you could see was smoke and flames. I thought, 'Lord, what is going to happen here?'

"When we drove through the central district of Newark, things had gotten so bad; Newark police community relations had deteriorated so much, people were out on their porches applauding us. 'Hooray! The troops have arrived. Everything will be fine. They will restore order.' Black folks were welcoming the troops in."

This welcoming attitude did not last long. Within days, Governor Hughes ordered the National Guard and the NJ State Police out of Newark. "When we left there," McLemore said, "we were like a dog with its tail between its legs. People threw piss at us." What accounted for the NJ State Police and the National Guard's precipitous fall from community grace?

Over months of investigation, the Lilley Commission took sworn testimony from more than 100 witnesses ranging from the Superintendent of the NJ State Police to Amiri Baraka, a poet and playwright whose activism had made him a frequent target for the local Newark police. After speaking with scores of Newark store owners and residents, the Commission concluded that members of both the police and the National Guard, motivated by racial prejudice, had used "excessive and unjustified force" on Newark residents and had specifically targeted African American-owned businesses for destruction. "These raids resulted in personal suffering to innocent small businessmen and property owners who have a stake in law and order and who had not participated in any unlawful act.

24

It embittered the Negro community as a whole, when the disorders had begun to ebb," the Commission concluded.

During the days of unrest, law enforcement and the National Guard claimed that they were fired on by snipers, whose shots led to the deaths of a Newark police detective and a Fire Captain responding to a fire call.[15] While not outright rejecting this claim, the *Lilley Report* noted the doubts of Newark's own police director at the time, Dominick Spina: "A lot of the reports of snipers was due to the — I hate to use the word — trigger-happy Guardsmen, who were firing at noises and firing indiscriminately, it appeared to me, and I was out in the field at all times."

McLemore's own experience shows how indiscriminate shooting by the police and National Guard resulted in dangerous "friendly fire" exchanges. He recalls walking in a patrol formation at dusk, when a streetlight came on and a Newark cop on patrol with him reflexively shot it out, prompting another patrol to blindly return fire in his direction. "It was the Keystone Cops. You had a situation where the National Guard and police were shooting at each other," he recalled.

Out of the 26 fatalities during the five days of unrest, 23 (including a number of innocent bystanders) were from gunshot wounds. The *Lilley Report* estimated that the National Guard and NJ State Police fired some 13,000 rounds in all. No total was available for the local police, who reported killing people — seven "justifiably" and three "by accident."

McLemore recalls he threw away ammunition rather than fire it. "I thought I was in a war," recalled the former Marine. "I never fired a shot, because I never saw anything to shoot at. I even threw away ammunition to show that I was involved, but I never fired my pistol or rifle."

The *Lilley Report* should be required reading today, but not just for its detailed summary of what happened during the five days of civil unrest in Newark. Like the Kerner Commission, which then-

President Lyndon Johnson created to look into the issue of urban unrest on a national scale, the Governor's Select Commission went into scrupulous detail to place the 1967 disturbances in historical perspective.[16] What became clear was that the police were imposing a kind of draconian law and order on the people of color in the city, while the political power structure that owned the police had turned the municipal government into an ongoing white-collar criminal enterprise.

The 200-page *Lilley Report* cast a critical eye on the City of Newark's economic and political power structure. It identified a widening gap between the white-dominated municipal government and the overwhelmingly Black electorate, whom the city's leaders were supposed to serve. It documented how African American businesses and local contractors were systematically excluded from public contracts, and it characterized the pervasive corruption of Newark's officialdom by quoting the words of one informant: "There is a price on everything in City Hall."

If further confirmation of the *Lilley Report*'s jaundiced view of Newark's elected leadership were needed, not long after the report was released the city's Mayor Hugh Addonizio was indicted and convicted on multiple corruption charges at a trial that linked him to organized crime.

For years the widespread self-dealing political corruption squeezed all it could out of Newark. The *Lilley Report* described a city that had the highest maternal and infant mortality rate in the nation, the highest rate of tuberculosis infection, and it ranked ninth out of 302 American cities in severity of air pollution. A half-century since the *Lilley Report* was issued, the COVID pandemic has driven home the enduring nature of those very same race-based economic and healthcare disparities that continue to define Newark, much of the State of New Jersey, and the entire nation.[17]

To this day, McLemore believes that, in the street chaos of the unrest of July 1967, there was at least one summary execution where a

26

Newark resident was shot multiple times by law enforcement without legal justification. To this day, the official cover story is that it was the NJ State Police and the National Guard that restored law and order. As the Addonizio conviction would reveal, the order they restored had little to do with the law.

Yet, those dark days in Newark in June 1967 — like the 1921 Tulsa Race Massacre, where a white mob killed scores of Black residents and looted and leveled hundreds of homes and businesses — would remain obscure for decades, even though it was part of Black America's lived experience. It's a tragic irony that the subtitle of the *Lilley Report* — more than 60 years ago — was *Report for Action*, because so much of what it describes as significant problems for Newark's population endure to this day and became even more evident during the pandemic. The *Lilley Report* cited a report from the period by the National Commission on Community Health Service that noted "the aggregate death rate in Newark…is 35 percent above the national standard, after full allowance for variations in composition of population by age, sex and race…".

Today in Newark — by every public health measure — even before COVID hit, health disparities have continued to manifest in elevated infant mortality and maternal morbidity, as well as chronic diseases like asthma and diabetes. "The City of Newark continues to display some of the worst health outcomes of any city in the United States," according to a 2016 report published by the New Jersey Health Care Quality Institute and the Nurse Practitioner Healthcare Foundation.[18] To this day, Newark still faces the challenge of an aging housing stock, low homeownership rates, and a lack of a sufficient inventory of quality, affordable housing.

The debate over our nation's public infrastructure is often limited to the elements in the to-do list compiled by the American Society of Civil Engineers every four years in their *Infrastructure Report Card*.[19] A more holistic approach would include a review of how past public infrastructure spending concretized our original sin of slavery. There's a glimmer of hope in seeing that the Biden administration is aware of how federal highway spending divided and decimated urban communities of color in places as geographically diverse as Los Angeles and Newark, New Jersey, and facilitated the white flight out of the cities to get a suburban mortgage with terms that Blacks were never offered.

Our violent racist past is still present and manifested in our existing plumbing. The images of long lines of residents in Flint, Michigan, and Newark, New Jersey, lining up for bottled water because their city water was contaminated with brain-damaging lead resembled what we once would have expected to see only in a *National Geographic* photo spread from a "developing nation."[20]

And yet, in the 21st century, Flint and Newark were not outliers. From coast to coast, from border to border, the threat of lead contamination is most pronounced in poor communities of color — with potentially devastating consequences for infants and children. The Centers for Disease Control warns that even a slight elevation of lead levels in the blood can reduce IQs, stunt development and lead to behavioral problems.[21]

In an academic whitepaper, entitled "The Racial Ecology of Lead Poisoning," Harvard researchers Robert Sampson and Alix Winter studied "the toxic inequality in Chicago neighborhoods from 1995 until 2013."[22] Sampson and Winter wrote, "Yet as the crisis in Flint, Michigan, revealed, there is a major health scourge that has not been subjected to the same analytic scrutiny at the neighborhood level as other health indicators — lead poisoning. Unlike longstanding health concerns, it was not until relatively recently that a sizable body of research built up and converged in concluding that lead is a major neurotoxin that impairs cognitive, physical, and behavioral functioning, even at relatively low levels." They flagged a National Research Council study from the late 1990s which asserted, "Science and society have been remarkably slow to recognize and respond to the full range of harm associated with lead exposure."

Lead can be found in water, in the air, and in the earth. Pathways to lead exposure include lead paint in aging and often abandoned housing stock, which proliferated after the 2008 Wall Street mortgage heist, particularly in poor and predominantly Black communities like Newark and Flint. Another source can be traced to the vast tracts of America's industrial wastelands left behind with reckless abandon by multinationals on their way to their next "host" community

28

As Reuters reported in May 2016, after the Flint water scandal broke, in the United States there were "nearly 3,000 areas with recently recorded lead poisoning rates at least double those in Flint during the peak of that city's contamination crisis…. And more than 1,100 of these communities had a rate of elevated blood tests at least four times higher."[23]

Reuters' map of the lead scourge extended "from Warren, Pennsylvania, a town on the Allegheny River where 36 percent of children tested had high lead levels, to a zip code on Goat Island, Texas, where a quarter of tests showed poisoning. In some pockets of Baltimore, Cleveland, and Philadelphia, where lead poisoning has spanned generations, the rate of elevated tests over the last decade was 40-50 percent." That report was based on the granular analysis of the data generated with neighborhood-by-neighborhood lead testing compiled by state health departments and the US Centers for Disease Control and Prevention.

As reported in 2019, in the journal *Health Affairs*, "there is no safe level of lead in the blood. [24] The effect of lead poisoning on major bodily systems is permanent, and no amount of clinical or public health intervention can reverse it." The journal continued, "For this reason, the American Academy of Pediatrics (AAP) has consistently recommended the adoption of health-based policies that require the identification of lead hazards before a child is exposed to them." [25]

This contaminated landscape is what you get when capital isn't held accountable and is given free range to take flight for its next temporary roost, leaving its toxic detritus behind. For decades across the country, even as our water supply systems have continued to deteriorate and schools have crumbled, government at all levels gave away billions in tax incentives and subsidies to corporations. [26]

Even as the Natural Resources Defense Council and the Newark Education Workers Caucus were warning officials about Newark's water and its dangerously elevated lead levels, Newark Mayor Ras Baraka and New Jersey Governor Phil Murphy, both identified as progressive Democrats, were offering Amazon $7 billion in incentives to locate in Newark.[27] "New Jersey is open for business, and now more than ever, Newark is the clear choice as the next presence for

Amazon corporate offices," said Murphy. "Amazon now has the opportunity to join in Newark's story of a city on the rise."

"Given the city and state's assets — a strong talent pipeline, a diverse tech base, unmatched infrastructure, and a highly accessible location — we are well poised to accommodate" the giant online retailer, Baraka told *Barron's*. That $7 billion offered by one medium-size state to one company would be about 20 percent of the $35 billion it would take to replace all the lead water pipes in the *entire nation*.

While we debate the issue of infrastructure, it can't exclude an honest inventory of how our past infrastructure choices reflect a systemic racist neglect that continues to threaten the lives of millions of children of color to this very day. Consider the research cited by Sampson and Winter that "nationwide, close to a third of Black children born between 1985 and 2000 were raised in a high-poverty neighborhood, compared to just one percent white."

I have been tracking environmental racism going back to my earliest work at *The Village Voice*. In my 1993 investigative feature, "The Uptown Flush — Cleaning up the Hudson, Fouling Up Harlem," I looked at the racist legacy of Robert Moses and how it helped land a massive sewer plant up in West Harlem, further burdening with additional air pollution a neighborhood already struggling with off-the-charts asthma rates.

Whenever a catastrophic climate event like Hurricane Sandy hit, I would make it my first order of business to go to places like Paterson, New Jersey (where I was born), and walk along River Road and interview the homeowners, tenants, and small business owners who were in a world of harm after the Passaic River had jumped its banks, ruining what they had built against all the racist odds they endured.

In preparation for covering the 2016 Presidential Election, I took a detailed look at how the two cities that were going to host the two major parties' conventions had fared after eight years of Obama's "hope and change." In Cleveland, so pivotal in Obama's Ohio win, the downtown was enjoying a robust revitalization; but there were also vast swaths of the rest of the community in which factory buildings were vacant. There were close to 6,000 <u>zombie homes</u> — homes that their owners believed were in foreclosure, even though the bank that holds their mortgages never completed the legal process to foreclose — a physical legacy of the foreclosure crisis which was still felt here. Some 20,000 had already been torn down, and for the homeowners in the poorer part of town, property values had dropped by as much as 80 percent.

In the years since, I have witnessed a grassroots movement taking hold that aims to hold banks — as well as local, state, and federal governments — accountable for decades of race-based, predatory mortgage practices. It's no coincidence that the same zip codes most vulnerable to flooding and industrial hazards are those communities of color that have been most devastated by COVID. Supporting local efforts to uplift these places is the most direct way to heal our nation. After all, what is a nation but a collection of specific places?

The Great Reconciliation — to get our nation "unstuck" — will require that we track the path that systemic racism and corporate greed have physically manifested through the national landscape, leaving so many communities with gaping wounds that endure to this day. If we are to be "Repairers of the Breach," as suggested by folks like Reverend Barber, we will need a roadmap to triage where the damage and suffering are most acute.

Chapter 2: Facing a Moral Understanding of Our History

We are adrift in the sea of time, with nothing but the stars and planetary alignments to chart our way. Where we are is relative to where we were, but so much of our essential past can be hiding in plain sight or just beyond our lived comprehension.

Consider a mass death event, like the 1918-1920 "Spanish Flu" pandemic. Hardly ancient history. Yet, until COVID-19, it remained an obscure tangent for academics about which a small group of people knew a lot but most of us remained clueless. Just a century ago, it was a traumatic event that rocked the world, killing 50 million people on the planet and 675,000 here in the United States. It infected 500 million people; yet, with the passage of time, it floated out to sea beyond the charts of our lived experience. That is, of course, until hundreds of thousands of Americans started dying from COVID.

Fortunately for humanity, history is not a static thing. It's a living, breathing social construct that can be an open-ended, dynamic conversation — if we have the moral courage to have it. Our understanding of history, though, depends on whose version we are reading (or being told) and how much time we spend reflecting on "how we know what we know." All stories come with the baked-in perspective — "framing" — of the storyteller.

So far, the American story has been used by institutional storytellers as a way of reaffirming the "greatness" of our founding white men, memorialized in oil as the signatories to our Declaration of Independence and the Framers of our Constitution. This ancestor worship has been spun, one generation after another, as the foundation for the article of faith that we were in an ever-forward path of progress in the pursuit of "a more perfect union." Yet, in this storytelling, we had not expiated the "original sin" of slavery that tainted our perfection.

And then came 2008. In the immediate aftermath of the election of President Barack Obama, a Gallup poll found a state of near euphoria among the public — with 70 percent of the people polled saying his election was a fulfillment of our hopes for improved race relations.

Unfortunately, seven years later in 2015, a New York Times/CBS poll found a much more pessimistic outlook.[28] One of the more revealing results from that survey was on attitudes about the Confederate battle flag: 57 percent of the white people surveyed said they viewed the flag as merely "an emblem of Southern pride;" as contrasted with 68 percent of African Americans, who said it was a symbol of racism.

It's in these divergent views toward that historic symbol that America's fractured narrative — torn apart more than 150 years ago and never reconciled — becomes clearer. So how do we stitch this gaping wound that resists healing? It starts by coming to terms with the specific brutality that was slavery, not by discharging its moral burden as though it evaporated with past generations.

For centuries, we have failed to directly address these crimes against humanity that were the cornerstones of American capitalism and are part of the continuum that extends systemic racism to our current circumstance. There is a direct through-line from slavery and the failure of Reconstruction to a "police riot" in 1967 Newark and the unfinished work of ensuring Equal Rights under the law, to the persistent racial-profiling bias exemplified in George Floyd's murder in 2020, right up to today's disproportionate impact of COVID on "essential workers" who are disproportionately people of color.

To expiate the original sin of American slavery, we have to own it. We don't get a pass because the slave owners are all dead and buried, even as the nation rests on the slabs of the very foundations they built.

As a kid growing up in New Jersey, I was taught in school that slavery was a Southern moral defect. Imagine my surprise when, at almost 60, I learned that my own state was once an enthusiastic booster of slavery. My path to enlightenment started while I was helping my oldest daughter, an organic farmer, at her stand at our local farmers' market a few years ago. The Mendham Farmers' Market was located on the Pitney Farm, which up until our town bought it a few years earlier (presumably to preserve it as common space) had been in the same family since the 1740s — 11 generations dating back to when New Jersey was a colony.[29]

As I stuffed kale into bags, I spotted a black-faced lawn jockey statue, which stood in front of the Pitneys' manor house, the architectural focal point of the old farmstead estate, surrounded by barns and additional cottages. I wondered: Was it possible that slaves worked this land? So I decided to do some research. And that's how the Pitney Farm became a prism of place through which I could glean the reality of slavery in my own community.

There was no mention of such history in any of the local literature, nor in the municipal documents that were part of the town's due diligence when it purchased the Pitney estate. Out back, the paint has faded on the "Bicentennial Farm" sign affixed to one of the red barns, vestiges of what was once a working farmstead. There's no marking to note that slaves were part of the life of this place — although I would come to learn that they were. In fact, slaves were a critical part of the economy throughout all of Morris County and across the entire state of New Jersey, from its earliest white settlement up until the end of the Civil War.

Back in 2008, before it moved to buy the property, Mendham Township commissioned a report from the Cultural Resource Consulting Group, with the remit of cataloging what was known about the historical significance of the site. The seven-page report highlighted the accomplishments of the Pitney family, which can trace its roots back to the area since before the American Revolution. Mahlon Pitney, one of the family's patriarchs, fought alongside George Washington at the Battle of Long Island in 1776. Another

35

Mahlon Pitney served two terms in Congress and was nominated by President Howard Taft to serve on the United States Supreme Court. From the CRCG report, we know the farm grew to encompass more than 700 acres and included a dairy operation. But the slaves were invisible in this analysis.

The Pitney Farm was the center of a hub of productive activity that included an iron forge and distillery. Pitney peaches and apple brandy were famous in their day. The place was prominent enough that it was a stop on the Rockaway Valley Railroad line that ran from Whitehouse Station in Hunterdon County to Morristown back in the late 19th century. The CRCG analysis concludes that the Pitney site has a multilayered historical significance because the 12-acre farmstead "demonstrates the evolution of the multigenerational homestead of an important and influential family that traces its roots to the Revolution" and that "distinguished themselves in the area of local, state, and federal law."

As for the day-to-day life on the colonial farm that laid the foundation for the family's commercial and civic achievements, though, the report claimed that not much is known. "Little information was uncovered concerning the family's farming activities during the mid to early 18th century," according to the CRCG report prepared by Gregory Dietrich, senior architectural historian.

That document makes no reference to the well-documented role of slavery at the Pitney Farms. There were, however, multiple extant historical records available online and in the Morris County Library. As I discovered, they offered a multidimensional image of just how much Mendham, and indeed my entire state, was reliant on — and enmeshed in — the day-to-day brutality of slavery.

My first break came while looking in a Rutgers University index for old court records online. I found that, in May of 1793, in the case "of Negro James, a Boy about Thirteen Years of age, claiming his freedom," New Jersey's Supreme Court ordered that James Pitney, listed as the defendant, "discharge" the Black teen from "illegal detention."[30] According to the history of the case, as recounted in the court order, three years earlier Pitney bought the enslaved boy from relatives of Jasper Smith of Hunterdon County. Smith had died in 1769 but in his will called for the freeing of "all my negroes,"

36

including "Negro Juddy," the mother of the boy now in Pitney's possession. (Evidently Smith's heirs had other ideas, and instead had sold James to Pitney.)

The order continues: "The Court having taken due consideration, are unanimously of Opinion, that the said Negro Juddy" was "a free woman by the Will of the said Jasper Smith which in turn meant that Juddy's son James was, as the State's highest court saw it, "entitled to his freedom."

Just four years later, that same Supreme Court, in a very similar habeas corpus petition, brought this time on behalf of a Native American known to the court only as "Rose," had a very different ruling that would keep her in slavery. "They [the Native Americans] have been so long recognized as slaves in our law," the Court wrote, "that it would be as great a violation of the rights of property to establish a contrary doctrine at the present day, as it would be in the case of Africans; and as useless to investigate the manner in which they originally lost their freedom." In that ruling the state's high court had internalized the Doctrine of Christian Discovery[31], promulgated by Pope Nicholas V in 1452, that gave Europe's monarchs the franchise to conquer and subjugate[32] the non-Christians inhabiting the planet, so as to add to the dominion of the Church.

In 1823, the United States Supreme Court ruled in Johnson v. M'Intosh that this grim franchise granted to European sovereigns had been transferred to the United States: "The United States, then, have unequivocally acceded to that great and broad rule by which its civilized inhabitants now hold this country. They hold and assert in themselves, the title by which it was acquired. They maintain, as all others have maintained, that discovery gave an exclusive right to extinguish the Indian title of occupancy, either by purchase or conquest; and gave also a right to such a degree of sovereignty, as the circumstances of the people would allow them to exercise."[33]

According to the late Rutgers professor Dr. Clement Price, "support for the institution" of slavery "was stronger in New Jersey than in any other northern colony." In 2008, on the occasion of the New Jersey State Legislature's formal apology for slavery, Price told the public television program "Due Process" that "slavery was very important to New Jersey's colonial economy."

From its founding, when it was called the "New Netherlands" as a Dutch colony in the early 1600s, and even after English successors re-named it "New Jersey," promoting slavery was hardwired into the state's political economy. According to the New Jersey State Library's Unit on African American Slavery in the Colonial Era, the colony's first constitution, the Concessions and Agreement of 1654/1665, actually "provided additional acreage" for each slave a prospective settler had.[34]

By the end of the 17th century, Jersey-bound settlers were promised between 60 to 75 acres for each slave they had on hand. Other documents indicate as much as a 150-acre incentive per slave. "The earliest known record of slaves in New Jersey dates to 1680, when Colonel Lewis Morris of Shrewsbury, Monmouth County, is identified as owning approximately sixty to seventy slaves," according to the New Jersey State Library.

Morris' holdings in Monmouth County included an ironworks and forge, which was the first constructed south of New England to reach the production stage. "It was structured as a plantation, and there were 60 or more slaves at the ironworks in 1680; the first notable instance of slavery on record in New Jersey," according to the Tinton Falls website.[35] Colonel Morris' nephew and heir, also named Lewis, inherited his holdings and was named the first Royal Governor of colonial New Jersey in 1738. (It is for this Lewis Morris that the New Jersey county is named.) Throughout this colonial period, supporting slavery was a major driver of public policy, and slavery was legally defined as including "negro, Indian, and mulatto slaves," according to Henry Scofield Cooley's "A Study of Slavery in New Jersey," published by the Johns Hopkins Press in 1896.[36]

In the early 1700s, the ongoing chronic shortage of manual and skilled labor for an expanding empire prompted Queen Anne to order that "a constant and sufficient supply of merchantable negroes" be available "at moderate rates" to New Jersey settlers. The Crown also wanted to ensure that there were no "encroachments" on the slave-trading franchise enjoyed by the Royal African Company by any enterprising locals.

While the first large-scale use of slaves has been traced to the Morris ironworks in southern Burlington County, slavery really gained

38

traction in the northern and eastern portion of New Jersey. The major slave port of entry for the slave traffic in New Jersey was through Perth Amboy. From 1737 until 1800, the slave population went from just under 4,000 to well over 12,000. By far the highest concentration of slave labor was in Bergen County, where by 1800 there were close to 3,000 slaves, almost 20 percent of the population.

Yet even as commercial interests embraced slavery, there was a countervailing movement for abolition in New Jersey. In 1693, Quakers out of Philadelphia, whose influence extended through southern and central New Jersey, issued the first anti-slavery pamphlet in North America. For the entirety of the time that slavery was countenanced by law, a vigorous debate raged in New Jersey that divided religious congregations throughout the state. During the American Revolution, the Reverend Jacob Green, a Morris County preacher, used the tumult of the times as a powerful rhetorical opportunity to call for abolition. As it turned out, the fault line of this great national debate ran right through my own home county.

The most obvious extant clue living in the landscape was the way some churches would incorporate the "first" or "second" in their name along with the denomination with little explanation. According to historian David Mitros, Reverend Green, who established the First Presbyterian Church of Hanover, was the first New Jersey man to publicly call for America's separation from Great Britain. In his book *Jacob Green, and the Slavery Debate in Revolutionary Morris Count*, Mitros writes that Green, in the darkest days of the Revolution, also warned from his pulpit that the nascent nation risked appearing a great hypocrite if it maintained slavery at its inception.[37]

"What foreign nation can believe that we who so loudly complain of Britain's attempts to oppress and enslave us," Green said, "are at the same time, voluntarily holding multitudes of fellow creatures in abject slavery... [even as we declare] that we esteem liberty the greatest earthly blessing." This sermon was published in 1779 as a pamphlet by the *New Jersey Journal* and helped frame the debate around the apparent contradiction of maintaining slavery while proclaiming national liberty.

From slavery's inception in New Jersey, slaves were subject to a separate set of laws and courts that had the power to dispense brutal punishment for any infractions. "In contrast to New England's liberal laws, the slave codes of New Jersey and other middle colonies resembled those of the South," writes David Mitros in his comprehensive *Slave Records of Morris County, NJ (1756-1841).*[38] "Judged in separate courts with no access to trial by jury, Blacks and American Indians accused of crimes in colonial New Jersey had little hope of receiving justice," writes Mitros. "When a slave received the death sentence, the slave owner received monetary compensation from the state."

In April 1712, two dozen armed African American slaves teamed up with Native Americans and set fire to a building in New York City and attempted to fight off the efforts to extinguish the fire. The slave rebellion was suppressed by a militia, and 21 of the slaves were executed, some by being burned at the stake. In reaction, both New York and New Jersey made their existing slave codes even stricter. In 1735, a slave in Bergen County, who was alleged to have tried to set a house on fire, was also burned at the stake. In 1741, two slaves in Hackensack charged with a similar crime met the same fate.

In 1743, a slave insurrection on the scale of the one in New York City was planned for Burlington County, but because the plan was foiled before it could be executed, only one suspect was hanged. "The rest were sentenced to be flogged or have their ears cut off," writes Maggie MacLean on her History of American Women blog.[39]

During the American Revolution, the British offered slaves their freedom in exchange for fighting for the Crown, and thousands of African Americans took them up on the offer. In New Jersey, the state itself sold the slaves they confiscated from loyalist sympathizers. In 1786, while the state banned the importation of slaves, it prohibited free Black people from moving into the state.

As brutal as the slave codes were, there was some effort in New Jersey to regulate potential abuses by the slave masters. In December of 1808, Mahlon Pitney, James's son, was the foreman on a Morris County jury of 12 men that convicted Abraham Cooper of Chester for using a hot iron to brand the forehead of his slave Cato. The jury ruled Cato was "thereby grievously wounded and hurt" and was put "to great pain, torture and other wrong" and fined Cooper $40, recounts David Mitros, in his *Slave Records of Morris County, NJ (1756-1841)*.

Four years after that, Mahlon Pitney registered with Morris County the birth of a female slave child named Peg, born on September 20, 1810, in Mendham to "my negro slave named Rachel," to comply with New Jersey's Gradual Abolition Act of 1804. That act mandated that children born to slaves born after July 4, 1804, would eventually be granted their freedom — for boys, only after they served for 25 years as slaves to their mother's master; for girls, that age was set at 21. Of course, the structure of the Gradual Abolition Act of 1804 required that thousands of African American women would give birth to children that would start their lives as slaves. It also had a provision for slave owners to "abandon" these children a year after their birth to the "county poorhouse," where they would be declared a pauper and "bound out" as indentured servants to the highest bidder by the overseers of the poor "in the same manner as other poor children."

"Some slave owners took full advantage of the law," writes Mitros. "They abandoned the slave children, then bid them back to receive the state "subsidy" for maintaining these "paupers," which got them $3 a month for their maintenance from the state treasury. Eventually this self-serving practice was ended in 1811, because it was consuming too much of the state's revenue.

New Jersey fought on the side of the Union in the Civil War. But, according to Jim Gigantino, professor of history at the University of Arkansas, New Jersey was the most enthusiastic Northern state when it came to holding on to slavery years after other Northern states had abolished it. In fact, before the end of the Civil War, New Jersey even voted down the 13th Amendment that would abolish slavery, only voting to ratify it in 1866, after the end of the Civil War and Lincoln's assassination months earlier.

Gigantino, who wrote *The Ragged Road to Abolition: Slavery and Freedom in New Jersey 1775-1865*, says that after the Civil War, New Jersey obscured its well-established support of slavery by choosing to "memorialize things about the end of slavery. [40]

"So, when we talk about slavery in modern times, we talk about emancipation or abolition of slavery," Gigantino says. "This is a purposeful reinvention of New Jersey as part of the free North narrative of participation in the underground railroad, participating in this freedom process." Professor Gigantino says his new research indicates that as many as 400 African Americans remained in some form of slavery at the end of the Civil War, not the reported 18 that were long accepted in the historical record. Recording numbers without names makes it easier to deflect moral obligation.

That's why I spoke up for the preservation of Pitney Farm at a 2015 Mendham Township Committee meeting, when they were considering selling off the property for private development. I felt we needed to know more about that "Negro James, a Boy about Thirteen Years of age" who claimed his freedom in 1793, according to the New Jersey Supreme Court's order requiring that James Pitney "discharge" the Black teen from "illegal detention." I hoped that the municipal government would consent to an archeological dig, so that we could possibly learn more about the slave experience that had been so long suppressed. Many other local residents supported that idea.

My request never came to pass. There was no official interest in digging up or referencing the past if it meant owning the town's historic role in slavery. (Coincidentally, it also might have encumbered any future development on the site if it was found to have some historic-preservation significance.) On a wet and wintry night in February 2016, the Pitney Manor House was gutted by a fire. The Morris County Prosecutor determined that it was arson. No one was held responsible. The local government subdivided and sold off much of the estate. It's one of the things we do best in New Jersey.

Chapter 3: Ignoring the Ignoble

To this day, there is an enduring American proclivity for ignoring the ignoble, the vengeful, cruel and corrupt that are woven into our national character. Our corporate media airbrushes our history, and we wonder why we just can't seem to master our destiny. There can be no forward motion, because we fail to perceive just how deep a rut we are in. We cling to the persistent delusion of American exceptionalism, despite all the physical evidence to the contrary — like having the worst response to the COVID pandemic in the world, with four percent of the world's population, but one-fifth the virus fatalities as of the beginning of 2021.

This was brought home to me — before the pandemic — on what had been my daily commute from Hoboken into the World Trade Center. Climbing up the depths of the underground rail platforms, I would pass through the then-tourist-packed space in my worker-drone state through what was Ground Zero, the site where 2,606 people perished. The site had been transformed into a glistening white-marble transit hub of massive cathedral proportions, erected as an homage to luxury goods. The scents of high-end female fragrances and expensive leather were infused with the aroma of Italian coffee and French pastries.

On this particular day, I was with a commuting buddy who was an architect. As we came to the center of the massive atrium called the Oculus, designed by Santiago Calatrava, I asked my architect friend for his assessment of the setting. "You mean this $4 billion boondoggle? This design is empty. It is just a shrine to shopping," he said. And it occurred to me that he was right. This vacuous, post-9/11 public work reflected the actual state of the soul of our nation

— big, empty, defined by consumption — a country that would have Donald Trump as its president.

Just as there had been no clue of the enslaved misery hiding in Pitney Farm's Mendham landscape, here at Ground Zero there was no hint of the massive human devastation on the day the Twin Towers fell. And, of course, there was no sign of the mega-death inflicted on the world since then, after America declared a "war on terrorism" in the Muslim world. And incredibly, the reality that many years later a massive lie by the Bush administration back in 2001 was still killing Americans here at home weekly.

Standing there, smelling the best that capitalism had to offer, you could be oblivious to the concentric seismic circles of death and destruction that our vengeful global war would set off a world away. Floating on a Hermès cloud, insulated from the nations we destabilized, it was impossible to hear the grotesque sounds of the worst refugee crisis since World War II that we had helped set in motion.

In March 2015, Physicians for Social Responsibility released a detailed study of 10 years of civilian casualties from our War on Terror, reporting that one million had been killed in Iraq, 220,000 in Afghanistan, and 80,000 in Pakistan. And those numbers don't include the subsequent slaughter that's playing out in Syria and Yemen or calculate the lost opportunity cost to a generation of children whose entire lives have been lived in the margins of armed conflict and displacement. So, for all these years since 9/11, our Congress has been — with a few exceptions — on autopilot, passing one massive military spending bill after another, not taking notice that we were funding "tens of thousands of ghost soldiers" in Afghanistan, according to the Office of the Special Inspector General for Afghanistan.

When four American soldiers were killed in the ambush in Niger in 2017, US Senators confessed their ignorance about that deployment. "I didn't know there were 1,000 US troops in Niger," Senator

Lindsey Graham told NBC's Chuck Todd. Graham went on to say the military had to be more forthcoming with Congress, "because this is an endless war without boundaries, with no limitation on time or geography."

Perhaps it was where my daily commute always landed me that had so alienated me from Calatrava's white-marble Fabergé egg. Maybe it was also just how much I knew about the behind-the-scenes corruption of the Port Authority of New York and New Jersey — the owner and developer of the site — which I had shorthanded over the years as the Hudson bi-state hustle, an ongoing criminal enterprise.

Just a few blocks away, the 277 Broadway offices of *The Chief-Leader*, the city's civil-service newspaper — and my workplace — were just about as different an environment as you could imagine. If One World Trade was about moving on from the ravages of 9/11, it was *The Chief-Leader*'s core mission to never forget. For the staff, 9/11 was not a discrete event that produced a static body count, but an ongoing story that was still claiming the lives — years later — of those that had succumbed to the diseases they got working and living around the WTC pile.

Stacks of yellow newsprint with faded headlines offered detailed accounts of lost history, like the paper's Friday, September 21, 2001, edition, with its headlines recounting the scale of the FDNY's massive death toll ten days earlier. The voices of the WTC walking wounded could often take physical form over the phone or in person, when they were looking for help from the newspaper to expose a brutal bureaucracy that wanted these people buried before they were dead.

The Chief-Leader was established in 1897, and it has provided generations of New Yorkers with the bureaucratic schematics on how to secure a civil-service job and how to climb that ladder once you got in. The paper was started 14 years after the enactment of the Pendleton Civil Service Act, signed into law by President Chester A. Arthur as a good-government reform designed to shift federal hiring away from a process rooted in political patronage to one informed by merit-based testing.

The paper's advertisers included workers' compensation lawyers whose practices included representing public employees that had

45

been injured on the job. *The Chief* offered its readers a glimpse behind the scenes of contract negotiations between their union and the City of New York and often included reporting on the level of risk attached to the various civil-service titles which could be monetized. As a consequence, it was *The Chief-Leader* that carried the earliest reports about the toxicity of the air that persisted in Lower Manhattan and western Brooklyn in the days and months after the 9/11 attacks.

Three days after the 9/11 attack, it was former New Jersey Governor Christine Todd Whitman, then head of the Environmental Protection Agency, who told reporters that "the good news continues to be that air samples we have taken have all been at levels that cause us no concern." That upbeat and inaccurate statement was uttered as the fires at the World Trade Center site continued to burn and smolder, as they would for months after the Towers collapsed.

No doubt, Whitman's reassurance and the encouraging EPA press releases — along with then-Mayor Rudolph Giuliani's cheerleading — helped Wall Street and Lower Manhattan's businesses and schools get back up and running so quickly. Within a few years, though, the revelation began to sink in that the danger had not passed, as thousands were becoming sick and dying from their exposure to the unique cocktail of abrasive toxins released by the collapse and fires that followed.

Two years after 9/11, an investigation by the EPA Inspector General found that EPA "did not have sufficient data and analyses to make such a blanket statement," as "air monitoring data was lacking for several pollutants of concern."[41] Moreover, the Office of Inspector General learned that it was President George W. Bush's White House Council on Environmental Quality (CEQ) that heavily edited the EPA press releases "to add reassuring statements and delete cautionary ones."

The EPA's Inspector General (IG) found that the CEQ described the readings as just "slightly above" the limit, despite the reality that samples taken indicated asbestos levels in Lower Manhattan were between double and triple EPA's limit. And when the EPA's IG tried to determine who had written the press releases, they "were unable to identify any EPA official who claimed ownership," because

46

investigators were told by the EPA Chief of Staff that "the ownership was joint ownership between EPA and the White House" and that "final approval came from the White House."

"She also told us that other considerations, such as the desire to reopen Wall Street and national security concerns, were considered when preparing EPA's early press releases," according to the EPA's Inspector General.[42]

According to a 2008 case study by the Union of Concerned Scientists, the EPA press releases were also vetted by Bush's national security advisor.[43] "Unfortunately, the agency lacked authoritative information on which to base these claims, and internal agency data conflicting with this reassuring public posture were ignored. The EPA's press releases and public statements after 9/11 were vetted by then-National Security Advisor Condoleezza Rice, suggesting that the White House placed politics over science when communicating about ground zero's air quality."

For a number of years after the attack and "cleanup," which dosed potentially a half-million people with the WTC "Drano dust," the City of New York, then led by Mayor Michael Bloomberg, resisted any claims by 9/11 first responders that linked their respiratory diseases and cancers to the big EPA lie. The Bloomberg denial reached its nadir when, after the death of WTC responder NYPD Detective Jimmy Zadroga, Bloomberg insisted the ailing detective had died because he was a drug addict.

Ultimately, it wasn't until 2006 that a New Jersey coroner found that Zadroga, who had spent weeks on the WTC pile wearing just a flimsy paper mask, had actually died of heart and lung failure brought on by the chronic disease that compromised his vital organs as a consequence of his post-9/11 WTC exposure. Mayor Bloomberg apologized to the Zadroga family.

In 2016, former Governor Whitman told *The Guardian* she was "very sorry that people are dying, and if the EPA and I in any way contributed to that, I'm sorry. We did the very best we could at the time with the knowledge we had."[44]

47

In the two decades since, the toll from the WTC toxic exposures has continued to mount, with the post-9/11 death toll likely exceeding the almost 3,000 killed in the actual attack and collapse. To this day, more than 106,000 first responders and survivors are enrolled in the federally funded 9/11 WTC Health Program, with many of these participants suffering from multiple diseases and debilitating conditions. While close to 95 percent of the first responders are participating in the 9/11 WTC Health Program and getting screened every year, less than 10 percent of the 400,000 civilians are enrolled in the program.

The New York City Fire Department (FDNY), which lost 343 the day of the attack, has since lost more than 200 firefighters and fire officers to WTC-related cancers and other diseases. Union officials estimate another 6,500 active and retired FDNY personnel continue to battle a certified WTC condition, including cancer — roughly more than half of the 11,000 FDNY-connected personnel that served at the site.

In the summer of 2018, I was working on a 9/11 retrospective for WBGO-Newark Public Radio. I was struck by the atmosphere on the outdoor plaza of the fully reconstructed One World Trade Center building, not far from the two WTC memorial reflective pools. Tourists from all over the world strolled through a festive green market, stopping to take selfies. It is a world away from the 9/11 attack that leveled the Twin Towers and left a massive toxic debris field that contaminated Lower Manhattan's air south of Canal Street for several months.

The WTC visitors I encountered were well aware of the body count on the day of the 9/11 attack. But they were unaware of the ongoing WTC health crisis that still defines and ends so many lives prematurely, as a consequence of the officials who decided that a quick Wall Street rebound trumped being transparent about the risk to public health.

It would be just another example of profits over people — a lot of people — who can be disappeared.

Lotey Aldrich, a 24-year-old from northern England, was on her first visit to the World Trade Center site. She was unaware of the WTC's ongoing death toll. I asked her, "Are you aware that there are a lot of people that have gotten sick from 9/11 that are still dying?"

"No, I did not know that. It is quite shocking," she said. "I would not have known that. We are going to the museums and find out more about it."

For Carolyn Happy and her family, who moved into nearby Battery Park City in 2006, the events of 9/11 and the aftermath remain vivid. She said that for her and her neighbors, the redevelopment of the site is a bit surreal. "The juiciness of all this high-end retail does a very good job in putting a weird veneer over what happened here on September 11th," Happy said.

Press accounts focused on the heroics of the uniformed first responders and the need for them to get health screening, reinforcing the importance of them signing up for the WTC Health Program. Happy said she's not sure why such a small percentage of civilians have signed up, despite their exposure.

"One family that I am very, very close with — I am super sure, as is my friend, that her husband died from the psychological impact," she recalled. "He was already a fragile soul, and he was an at-home dad. And he had taken their daughter — who is now a senior in college — to nursery school on Greenwich, and he had my daughter's friend Jack in the BabyBjorn [carrier] when it happened. He and Jack were covered with that white dust, and Jack stopped breathing at some point. Fortunately, someone — another friend in the neighborhood — was like, 'I think Jack is not breathing,' and he got him out of the BabyBjorn. And they were able to, like, get him into one of the little supermarkets, and they used a lot of water to, like, revive him."

Happy was not surprised that tourists were not clued in about the ongoing WTC health crisis.[45] "I wouldn't be surprised at all that they don't have any idea of what that effect is and that it is still going on," she said. "I have a feeling that really the whole point of the 9/11 Memorial is to show how remarkable the recovery is and that we can't be broken; and we can't this and we can't that. I think if you were to include that there are still lingering side effects for a lot of

49

people who are going to die from painful illnesses, that doesn't sound as heroic, so back on our feet again."

In the summer of 2019, after months of contentious debate, Congress approved a permanent extension of the September 11th Victims' Compensation Fund, which offers cash awards for victims and their families. Lawmakers applauded Jon Stewart, the former "Daily Show" host, for his pivotal role in drawing attention to the plight of the police officers, firefighters, and others who had rushed to the WTC site to help, or assisted in the cleanup, but were later diagnosed with cancer and other diseases linked to their exposure to the toxic dust and fumes. After the vote, Stewart praised the first responders who testified alongside him as the true heroes of the legislative victory. Survivors, in turn, thanked legislative leaders for finally overcoming political obstruction and passing the law.

But once again, largely overlooked in the celebratory moment were the hundreds of thousands of people, some of whom were undocumented, who simply lived, worked, or went to school at or near the site. Many of them have also gotten sick and died in the months and years since 9/11, while many more have never even been screened for cancer, asthma, and other ailments linked to the attacks. Although these survivors are eligible for the WTC Health Program — the federal program that is now fully funded by Congress — it's much harder for them to benefit from it than for first responders. Outreach is spotty, allowing countless survivors to fall through the cracks. Some do not yet have any symptoms and may not know that their exposure could result in medical problems years later. And, unlike first responders, they're only eligible if they already have symptoms — at which point it may be too late to treat a condition.

Dr. Joseph Fennelly, who served for decades as the chairman or co-chairman of the Medical Society of New Jersey's bioethics committee, said that "from an ethical standpoint, there's no question" that survivors should have the same unfettered access as first responders to regular screening without having to be symptomatic as a prerequisite. "You absolutely want to try and catch cancers before they are symptomatic," he said. "This is part of the zeitgeist of medicine moving towards prevention."

Attorney Michael Barasch, a leading attorney representing 9/11 victims, agreed. "It's outrageous that the 400,000 civilians, including downtown office workers, residents, students, and teachers, are treated differently than the 100,000 first responders," he said. "After all, they were all breathing the same toxic dust. Not surprisingly, they are all being diagnosed with the same illnesses."

Barasch said that, without free annual checkups, many of these survivors won't learn about the risks they face. "As a result, most of them have no idea that there is a presumption linking 68 cancers to the toxins," he said. "If they don't see a doctor from the Health Program, they likely will never connect the dots. It's time to stop treating the survivors in the 9/11 community as second-class citizens."

Catherine McVay Hughes, a former chairwoman of Lower Manhattan's Community Board 1, which includes the WTC site, remembers being skeptical when former EPA Administrator Whitman proclaimed that air in Lower Manhattan was safe — even as the fires at the WTC site were burning and would not be fully extinguished until just before Christmas.[46] But Hughes, who serves on the WTC Scientific/Technical Advisory Committee, said that it was taboo at the time to raise such concerns. "First of all, I am one of the most patriotic people out there," said Hughes, who was speaking only as a longtime member of the community. "But questioning whether or not the air was safe to breathe back then was perceived as almost being unpatriotic; and nowadays, there's scientific studies indicating how toxic and dangerous it was."

Lila Nordstrom is one of the young adults who is enrolled in the WTC Health Program. She said she's very grateful for the peace of mind it brings her. She was a 17-year-old student at Stuyvesant High School on the day of the attacks in 2001. The school, which had about 3,000 students at the time, is a few blocks from the WTC site.

When classes resumed, she and her classmates were sent to another high school in Brooklyn. But that October, a few weeks after Whitman had declared that the air was safe to breathe, the students were sent back to Stuyvesant. While testifying this past June to a Congressional committee that was weighing reauthorization of the 9/11 Victims' Compensation Fund, Nordstrom recalled the "cryptic

51

warnings" not to use the water fountains and not to exit the building at all during the day, the "acrid smell of smoke" permeating the building, and an endless stream of trucks dumping debris from the site next to the school, with "clouds of dust" spiraling up and into the building's air intake system. "Suffice it to say, my lungs suffered; and I certainly was not alone," she said. "As soon as Stuyvesant students returned, there were widespread reports of nosebleeds, coughs that just wouldn't go away, chronic headaches, and students suffering from a slew of worsening respiratory issues."

After high school, Nordstrom went on to graduate from Vassar College. In 2007 she moved to California, where she struggled with her "out of control asthma." "My entire 20s were dominated by financial panic, because even asthma and GERD can be quite expensive to treat under our current healthcare system," Nordstrom testified. "Adding to that stress is the fact that doctors in California, where I live, have often never seen a 9/11 survivor and don't understand the unique health risks I face."

In 2006, Nordstrom founded "StuyHealth," a nonprofit that does WTC health education outreach to her peers. She now knows at least five classmates who have been diagnosed with lymphomas, one in remission from thyroid cancer, another in remission from testicular cancer. Other Stuyvesant alumni have been diagnosed with rare bone cancers, melanoma, and male breast cancer. "What the EPA knew, but we didn't, was that the air was not safe," she testified. "Now, in addition to the illnesses and deaths we're seeing among responders, the death toll from 9/11-related illnesses is also mounting among survivors; and new people continue to fall ill, many of them my age or younger."

Stuyvesant is only one of the public schools that New York City operated in the contamination zone in Lower Manhattan and part of Brooklyn. After the EPA's pronouncement that the air was safe to breathe, the city reopened 29 schools in the zone. They were attended by almost 20,000 students, and the United Federation of Teachers says there were 2,500 teachers and support staff working in those schools.[47]

At a New York City Council hearing in 2018, Ellie Engler, the UFT's top industrial hygienist at the time of the attack, blasted city government. "The Department of Education and the New York City Department of Health have done nothing — zero — to reach out to those kids, and that's what I ask you to do," said Engler, now an aide to UFT President Michael Mulgrew. A Department of Education spokesperson at the time of the hearing disputed Engler's assertions that the agency had not been proactive in advising students and their parents about their health risks.

Engler said that two of her former colleagues died from cancer; and in 2017, after years of respiratory issues, she was diagnosed with thyroid cancer. In her testimony, Engler said that after 9/11, a joint team from the public school system and the UFT inspected several schools that were "most directly in the path of the fallout," and that the city and union closely monitored the status of the cleanup as schools were reopened. However, she added, "It took years before any of us made a connection and understood the breadth of the health crisis that would befall many. Only as first responders started getting sick, with unusual cancers and multiple respiratory problems, did the real impact become public. The message had not hit home."

The UFT pressed the New York City Council to pass legislation requiring the Department of Education to work with the Department of Health and Mental Hygiene to submit a report on outreach efforts to former students and staff members from the schools in the contamination zone. One co-sponsor of the legislation, City Council Health Committee Chairman Mark Levine, said at a press conference in May 2019 that within weeks of the attack, public school employees, from principals to cafeteria workers, were back at work at dozens of schools "at enormous risk" to themselves. "Today, this date, this city has not prepared an accounting of the staff and students," Levine said. "We don't have a comprehensive list of who they are. We have not communicated to them to let them know about the health risks we now know are very real. We have not let them know about the services and the support that are available to them as people who were at risk during those dangerous days following 9/11."

For now, the health status of the thousands of children who attended the city's public schools in Lower Manhattan on 9/11 and the months following is largely unknown. The WTC Health Program has just 758 survivors registered who are under 35, approximately the current age of the oldest of the students who were in those schools in 2001.

Almost 20 years after the attack, there is still a lot that is unknown about the health of most of the people epidemiologists say were at risk from the toxic fallout.

Testifying before Congress in June 2019, Dr. Jacqueline Moline, the director of the Northwell Health Queens WTC Health Program, predicted the public health crisis has not yet peaked.[48] Moline said that the day would come when "there are more people that died of WTC-related diseases after 9/11 than perished that horrible day." Yet, as Moline explained in an online video[49] about advances in screening and treating survivors, there are two different World Trade Center Health Programs: one for first responders and another for survivors.[50] The first responders, who were involved in rescue, recovery, and debris removal, undergo medical and mental health screening, monitoring and treatment, but the "presence of symptoms is not necessary to be eligible for the program."

"Survivors include community members, local workers, building re-occupants, residents, students, and cleanup workers," Moline said. "Medical and mental health treatment is included for World Trade Center-related medical and mental health symptoms and cancers. Medical and mental health monitoring is available once people are enrolled in the program. However, it differs from the responders' program in that the presence of symptoms or cancers is necessary to be program-eligible."

Hughes, the former Community Board 1 chairwoman, offered two explanations for the disparity between first responders enrolled in the program and the share of survivors in their version of the program. "For the survivor population, it means stepping forward to engage, whereas if you were a first responder, like a firefighter or in the NYPD, your health was already being tracked," she said. "For some of the members of the survivor community, when there is a tragedy like 9/11, you think that other people may have been exposed more or are worse off; and that if there are limited resources, you want to make sure they got it, that they got what they needed."

Barasch, the attorney representing victims, said that most of the first responders he has spoken with told him they knew what they were signing up for when they participated in the rescue and recovery operations. "The survivors, on the other hand, did not know what they were signing up for when they believed the EPA's assessment that the air was safe and went back home, to school, and to work," Barasch said.

In her testimony to Congress, Nordstrom said that many of her classmates have long since moved to other parts of the country and are even less likely to learn about federal medical assistance for which they may qualify. "Young adults are also especially at risk of losing out on the [Victims' Compensation Fund] because we face some big obstacles to even finding out about the 9/11 health services," she said. "Many of us ... don't have access to local information about the VCF, don't see it reported on in local media, and don't have local advocates. This often seems to get lost in the conversation about who needs this program and why."

The disparity between the number of 9/11 first responders whose health was being closely monitored and that of civilian survivors took on an even greater gravity in the midst of the COVID pandemic, when public health officials warned that individuals with WTC-type cancers and respiratory conditions were at a significantly higher risk of dying from the coronavirus.

In late 2020, advocates for participants in the 9/11 WTC Health Program made their case for expediting access to the COVID vaccine for the first responders and civilian survivors suffering from multiple health conditions that make them far more susceptible. "We've heard from the experts at the last meeting of the World Trade Center Medical Advisory and Steering Committee the numbers they are seeing during the pandemic prove that WTC first responders and survivors are at a significantly higher risk for COVID complications," said retired Paramedic Gary Smiley, who is District Council 37's Local 2507 WTC ombudsman. "All of the members of our union that we lost to COVID were also WTC responders with significant WTC illnesses."

Almost a year into the pandemic, Nordstrom, the former Stuyvesant High School senior who founded StuyHealth, said getting access to the COVID vaccine for her fellow New York City students who were at risk due to 9/11 needed to be a priority. "I'd definitely support that [expedited access to the COVID vaccine], especially because many survivors are in states where the process is going to be unreliable and complicated," she said during a phone interview. "I've heard the same from responders. Also, many of us tend to have very long, complicated recoveries even from common colds, though I don't have data on specifics because...nobody does. It's been hard to go see doctors during this time."

Barasch said that during the pandemic he had already lost 120 of his WTC clients; "and in all cases, they had underlying respiratory issues and/or cancer, which compromised their immune system... The government lied to the 9/11 community about the quality of the air after 9/11, and as a result of that lie and broken trust, tens of thousands of first responders and civilians were all exposed to the same dust and illnesses," he said. "Don't make them suffer twice." And yet, they do suffer on the periphery of the news of the day. The rising tide of COVID's mass death is of such a scale that the 24/7 losses of life have become a blur.

In December 2020, Local 2507 union member Evelyn Ford, a 27-year veteran NYC Emergency Medical Services (EMS) dispatcher who was 58, became the fifth NYC EMS employee to die from the disease. She was also a participant in the WTC Health Program, as was her husband, Darnell Ford, a private-sector EMT at Jamaica Hospital, who died of COVID-19 in November 2020.

For 9/11 WTC first responders still on the job in the midst of the pandemic, there's a tragic parallel between the betrayal they experienced at the hands of a dishonest EPA in 2001, in order to reopen Wall Street, and the Trump administration's downplaying of the COVID virus in a bid to limit its impact on the financial markets in 2020. Except this time, it would be the public health of the entire United States that Trump would be putting at risk for Wall Street, in hopes that the markets' performance would help him hold on to power.

Every step of the way, once again, it would be the first responders and essential workers that would be caught in the switches and sacrificed. As with the lingering 9/11 aftermath, there will be an army of suffering COVID survivors that will be the living witnesses to his barbarism and the excesses of winner-take-all capitalism. Except this time, it won't be tens of thousands who are the walking wounded. It will be millions struggling with chronic COVID-related diseases, if they're lucky enough not to be killed by it.

Chapter 4: Applauding and Dismissing the Essential

One of the most pernicious characteristics of our "Stuck Nation" is that it will rhetorically glorify the people that serve and protect it yet simultaneously neglect and abuse them, especially if doing so helps keep great fortunes intact. Early on in the pandemic, there was an effusive appreciation for the work of first responders and other essential workers, for whom working remotely was not an option. Signs honoring nurses, postal workers, and grocery clerks popped up across the American landscape. There was talk of "hazard pay" for those who were putting themselves and their families at risk of catching the highly contagious and deadly virus. But the idea only got short-term traction and fizzled entirely when, at the end of Trump's tenure and in its last days of Republican control, the Senate stalled and ultimately passed a watered-down version of House Speaker Nancy Pelosi's second COVID relief plan.

In the weeks after President Biden's inauguration, the administration went through the motions of trying to engage Senate Republicans in its deliberations over the final form of the $1.9 trillion American Rescue Plan. On February 1, the day before Ground Hog Day, Biden met with 10 GOP Senators to discuss their $600 billion anemic counterproposal. At that point we knew that 530,000 of us had died; but, as with the US Postal Service, employers were reluctant to publicly disclose their body count for fear of incurring liability.[51] Close to 30 million had been infected at that point, with as many as one third of those survivors experiencing lingering symptoms of varying severity that could lead to permanent disability.[52] In the waning days of the Trump administration, progress had halted on aid to local, county, and state governments, as then-Majority Leader Mitch McConnell held out for a provision that would indemnify the nation's corporations from potential lawsuits brought by employees who had contracted COVID as a consequence of workplace exposure due to their employers' failure to provide sufficient protections.

Even before the pandemic hit, if Upton Sinclair were to write the modern equivalent of "The Jungle," he might make the setting the metaphorical meat grinder of today's emergency medical services industry. Across the nation, emergency medical service professionals, the front-line workforce upon which so much of a patient's outcome rests, are grossly underpaid for brutal work schedules that put them at risk of both serious physical injury and burnout. The cherry on top of this abuse sundae is that they are 14 times more likely to be violently assaulted on the job than a firefighter.[53]

In 2017, FDNY Paramedic Yadira Arroyo was murdered on the job, allegedly by a homeless man with serious mental health issues.[54] In Summer 2019, a Boston emergency medical technician (EMT) survived after being stabbed multiple times.[55] These workers are in harm's way, yet they make nowhere near the income of their fellow first responders — namely, police officers and firefighters. And, like cops, EMTs are forced to deal with the people that much of society avoids: the homeless, the mentally ill, and folks in the throes of alcohol and drug addiction. Across the country, the everyday violence directed toward EMTs has led to some being issued body armor.[56] Yet, beyond this defensive protection, these healers have nothing to protect themselves from harm — aside from street smarts.

The irony is that, when emergency medical professionals respond to care for a patient, the clock starts running on what is dubbed the "golden hour," as much of a patient's long-term prognosis is dictated by what happens in those critical first 60 minutes and by the skill of the EMTs on the scene. Though the EMT's role is critical to public health, their pay is not commensurate. In an industry where the average CEO's salary is $16.1 million a year, up from $14.7 million just last year, these workers can make as little as $22,760 a year — or $11.38 an hour — according to the Department of Labor's Bureau of Labor Statistics.[57]

According to a survey by the Associated Press and Equilar, an executive search firm, the healthcare sector has thrown more money at its CEOs than any other sector, including energy and finance. Meanwhile, down here on Earth during a pandemic, the median EMT and paramedics wage was $34,320 in 2020. EMTs who work for a hospital make out the best, at $36,650; but private ambulance services lag behind, with a median salary of $31,590 for their workers, according to the DOL's Bureau of Labor Statistics.[58] The gender pay gap is astonishing, too: In one national survey, male EMTs doing the same job as women were averaging $10,000 more per year.[59]

The low pay, the long hours, even compulsory overtime — along with the stress that comes with having to be ready for anything — take a serious toll that puts both the EMS workforce and their patients at risk.[60] The sector is plagued with high turnover and chronic short-staffing — which leads to more mandatory overtime, workplace injury and burnout, or worse.

"Do this math, and you'll find some crews may not stop during their entire 24-hour shift," reported trade publication *EMS World* in its March 2019 issue. "Half of EMS personnel sleep only six hours every 24, with more than half reporting poor sleep quality and 70 percent reporting some problems with sleep. Loss of sleep, stressful situations, and not eating on a regular schedule could push an already-stressed employee close to the edge."

The analysis continued, "Insufficient sleep has been linked to cardiovascular disease, obesity, metabolic disorders, gastrointestinal conditions, hunger/appetite, and changes in emotion. Research has found higher levels of negative behavior correlating to sleep deprivation and that a person going without sleep for 24 hours experiences impairment equivalent to a blood alcohol of 0.10 percent."

As it turned out, long before COVID, the front lines of America's healthcare system were staffed by lots of people struggling to make ends meet in an occupation where one mistake means someone

61

might die. "In 2014 the Bureau of Labor Statistics reported the overall injury rate for EMTs and paramedics was 333 injuries per 10,000 workers — more than three times higher than the average rate of 107 for all occupational groups in the US," according to *EMS World*. But getting hurt on the job is the least of it.

According to a National Institutes of Health research paper published in May 2019, national survey data indicate "that among Emergency Medical Technicians (EMTs), including firefighters and paramedics, rates of suicide are significantly higher than among the general public.[61] EMTs face high levels of acute and chronic stress as well as high rates of depression and substance abuse, which increase their risk of suicide."

This cycle of pain, misery, and loss is what you get when the organizing principle of your healthcare system is not human wellness, but unfettered greed. With the pandemic, there was suddenly a shift in at least the public's perception of which workers were essential for society to continue functioning. EMTs, historically underpaid to rescue humans at their greatest hour of need, were now on the front line and were some of its first casualties.

For years, the unions that represent EMTs have warned that the American Emergency Medicine System has long been the weakest link in our healthcare system, upon which COVID-19 has been placing an unprecedented strain.[62] While police and firefighting services are universally accepted as part of our municipal social contract, the same is not true for emergency medical services. Americans in rural and suburban communities often rely on voluntary ambulance corps, which suffer from a chronic personnel shortage. Other regions are reliant on predatory for-profit companies that pay EMTs fast-food wages but charge exorbitant fees to patients.

As NBC reported in 2019, in a story entitled "What if you call 911 and no one comes? Inside the Collapse of America's Emergency Medical Service," just 11 of the nation's 50 states require by statute the establishment of a local EMS department.[63] Decades of shortsighted, profit-driven healthcare policies have closed scores of hospitals — a trend also well documented in urban communities of color.[64] That was one of the factors that made this pandemic particularly devastating in the United States.

Burnout, injury, and turnover rates are high among EMTs, even among the better-paid civil-service EMS units that are more common in big cities.[65] As a consequence, EMTs often end up leaving long before they hit the six-year tenure mark, which is when peer-reviewed medical studies indicate their patients have better outcomes.[66]

"This is a serious issue throughout the entire country," said Oren Barzilay, president of the national EMS Labor Alliance and New York City District Council 37's Local 2507, which represents the FDNY's EMS and EMT paramedics. "We don't have voluntary police departments across our country, and it's a good thing; otherwise, we would have chaos.... EMS has been in crisis for a long time, and the COVID-19 epidemic exposes that," Barzilay continued. "There needs to be national guidelines demanding we have an organized EMS workforce, like we do for police and fire. Just in New York State over the past year, we have seen EMS companies go out of business and so many of the voluntary EMS houses all shut down because there are no more volunteers," Barzilay said.

Perhaps no facet of our national for-profit healthcare system is more patchwork and dysfunctional than EMS. For whatever reason — perhaps because EMTs often wear blue collars or have lower social status and lower pay than fellow first responders like firefighters or police officers — their plight is largely ignored. In Washington, D.C., the nation's firefighters have the influential International Association of Firefighters.[67] Police officers have a myriad of national professional organizations. Lobbyists for both of these branches of America's first-responder services ensure the needs of these professionals are on the radar of federal, state, county, and municipal elected officials.

Michael MacNeil is president of the EMS/BPPBA, which represents the 400 members of the EMS union that serves Boston. That bargaining unit has the rare distinction of having pay parity with other first responders. MacNeil told me that Congress needs to pass federal legislation immediately to provide local community block grants across the country to help reinforce existing EMS units. In addition, he says there needs to be a lead EMS agency, akin to the U.S. Fire Administration, which conducts critical national data collection and best-practices research and benchmarking for

63

firefighting.[68] "These are things our national EMS Labor Alliance has been pushing for a long time," MacNeil said.

MacNeil says the second urgent national action item, in light of COVID-19, is dismantling the reimbursement economics that force EMTs to take their patients to the emergency room in order for their agency to get paid, whether or not it's the right healthcare call for the patient. "There's a money attachment to the way we deliver this essential service," he said. "It all links back to Medicare, Medicaid, and private insurance reimbursements; and in places like New York City and Boston our services can generate money. But we need to see what we are doing in the community — whether it results in an ER visit or not — as part of protecting the public safety, like we do with cops and firefighters."

In Austin, Texas, where city officials on March 6, 2020, made the difficult decision to cancel the 34th annual South-by-Southwest Festival, the local EMS union has been an integral part of the city's efforts at a proactive COVID-19 response outside the hospital setting. Selena Xie is president of the Austin EMS Association, which represents 550 members who enjoy the same civil-service status as the city's police and firefighters, but provide a public safety net well outside the confines of the hospitals.

When the city decided to close its libraries and recreation centers as part of its social-distancing strategy, it was the members of the EMS Association, who serve as Community Health Paramedics and who specifically serve the city's 2,500 homeless people, that alerted officials to the unintended consequences for this vulnerable population. Suddenly, Austin's homeless community had nowhere to go. "The homeless had no access to cable news or iPhones, so for everything to close suddenly like that on them was really scary," Xie said. "We lobbied the city to open the libraries and rec center; and then we organized a community group that's providing 500 meals a day, while the city figures out how they are going to realign their pantries and [get] shelter-in-place worked out."

As Austin's example illustrates, it is at the granular, neighborhood level out in the community where the new battle lines for the COVID-19 war were being drawn. Mobile and engaged EMTs and paramedics helped quell the panic run to the hospitals, which became gravely overtaxed in many hard-hit jurisdictions. As crucial as the Austin EMS is to the medical community and the public health response to coronavirus, Xie said that they were completely invisible in the eyes of the local news media. "Our local news outlet talked about what police and fire were doing for COVID-19 and didn't even think to include EMS," she lamented.

Incredibly, despite the way that COVID has revealed just how degraded America's public health system had become after decades of disinvestment, the need to promote a well-funded and -trained Emergency Medical Service is not part of the Beltway debate about the size and shape of the Biden administration's infrastructure package. Of course, that can be traced back to the reality that, in a political system where the wealthy have an oversized role in government decision-making, something as vital and basic for the vast masses of the American people like EMS is simply ignored as a "local problem."

Chapter 5: Discounting, Disappearing, and Disenfranchising

That America's emergency medical service workers, who are so often women and people of color, should be paid so poorly is emblematic of an economy that puts profits over people, even when lives hang in the balance. It's the common thread woven into our vintage American fabric. Even the labor movement itself has struggled to come to terms with the structural sexism and racism that have been consistently present in the country since the nation's creation.

The circumstances of slaves, undocumented immigrants, and low-wage workers have been part of a cohort of humanity that has always been invisible to the powers-that-be. From America's colonial nascency, right up through 2020 when President Trump ignored the mounting body count of essential workers killed by the virus that his policies had helped spread, the economic system has been fueled by this group's sacrifice.

As discussed in Chapter 2, hard-wired into much of capitalism's groundwork are the structural racism and economic exploitation that have their roots in the Doctrine of Christian Discovery. This doctrine is a concept that has been described by the Upstander Project as "the spiritual, political, and legal justification for colonization and seizure of land not inhabited by Christians."[69] It dates back to "papal bulls" (or decrees), the most often cited being those promulgated by Pope Nicholas V in 1452 that gave Europe's monarchs the franchise to conquer and subjugate the non-believers inhabiting the earth, so as to add to the dominion of the church.

This Doctrine was advanced by the Catholic Church as a way of trying to reduce the conflict between the European monarchs who were all vying for a piece of the "discovery" action in the Americas, Asia, Australia, and New Zealand. "This ideology supported the dehumanization of those living on the land and dispossession, murder, and forced assimilation," according to the Upstander Project. "The Doctrine fueled white supremacy, insofar as white European settlers claimed they were instruments of divine design and possessed cultural superiority."

The foundation for today's rapacious multinationals, scouring the earth for profits and then stashing them in safe havens to avoid taxation, was established by early 17th-century trading companies like the East India, Hudson Bay, and Dutch East India Companies.

In the years that followed, American court rulings built a legal framework for a kind of slow-motion genocide of native peoples with the courts affirming over and over the arrangement which resulted in what the American Bar Association calls "the mass dispossession of Indian lands, exploitation of Indian resources by outsiders, and attacks on tribal cultures, governments, and economies."

As noted by historian Alan Taylor in his *American Republics: A Continental History of the United States, 1783–1850*, by the 1830s, the federal government was spending two fifths of its annual budget on fighting and removing Native Americans from their land. Similarly, while the United States Congress ratified the 13th Amendment to the Constitution in December of 1865 and freed the slaves, through a myriad of ways, the power structure has continued to exploit the labor of people of color while at the same time throttling their ability to participate in the democracy whose physical infrastructure they built.

"In each generation, new tactics have been used for achieving the same goals — goals shared by the Founding Fathers. Denying African Americans citizenship was deemed essential to the formation of the original union," writes Michelle Alexander in her seminal book *The New Jim Crow.*[70] "Hundreds of years later, America is not an egalitarian democracy. The arguments and rationalizations that have been trotted out in support of racial exclusion and discrimination in its various forms have changed and evolved, but the outcome has remained largely the same."

Throughout American history, even when there were socio-economic advances for white workers — as there were during the Franklin Delano Roosevelt administration, which mandated the eight-hour day — our political system found a way to exclude millions of people of color as it did in the 1930s by exempting domestic and agriculture workers from FDR's labor reforms. And so decades later, this discounting, disappearing, and disenfranchising has endured to this day in a new century alongside a hyper-capitalism where income and wealth inequality reach new heights with each passing year.

In his seminal speech to the Southern Christian Leadership Council in August 1967, Dr. Martin Luther King identified the cracks in our foundation. He said there was something that needed to be fundamentally questioned about a society that produced tens of millions of poor people of color, whose ancestors had "built the spanning bridges and grand mansions, the sturdy docks and stout factories of the South" and whose "unpaid labor made cotton 'King' and established America as a significant nation in international commerce." Dr. King continued, observing that even after their "release from chattel slavery" the nation went on to become "the richest, most powerful society in the history of man," but left behind entirely those who had actually built it for free and their descendants.

No doubt, such a pernicious economic system — fueled to this very day on such a race-based, economic exploitation — must be not only questioned, but dismantled. "And when you begin to ask that question, you are raising a question about the economic system, about a broader distribution of wealth," King said. "When you ask that question, you begin to question the capitalistic economy. We are called upon to help the discouraged beggars in life's marketplace. But one day we must come to see that an edifice which produces beggars needs restructuring."

Overlooking that exploitation is one of capitalism's most willful blind spots. But every so often, its excesses cannot be concealed from plain view. Such was the case 110 years ago, when 146 garment workers, including 123 young immigrant women, died in the Triangle Shirtwaist Factory fire in Lower Manhattan. The intensely anti-union sweatshop owners had insisted on keeping exits locked, and only one of four elevators were operating; so many of those women were forced to jump from several stories to their deaths on the pavement below.

These women were paid $15 a week and worked at least 12 hours a day, seven days a week. The owners of the sweatshop were outliers, who continued to resist the union that had been so effective during the citywide strike from November 1909 to February 1910, by winning better pay and a more humane work schedule industry wide. The very public and grotesque deaths on a city sidewalk of so many women, filled with all of the potentiality of youth, punctured the conscience of New York City and helped spark a national movement for unions, labor rights, and worker safety. A generation later, that movement would be foundational to President Franklin Delano Roosevelt's "New Deal."

The manslaughter trial of those sweatshop owners, Max Blanck and Isaac Harris — also known as the "Shirtwaist Kings" — resulted in their acquittal. Yet they were forever condemned in the court of public opinion, which was informed by the disclosure that they had previously had fires at that Triangle site and that their Diamond Waist Company plant had also burned twice before.

In the years since, the Triangle Fire Coalition and the New York Central Labor Council of the AFL-CIO have held an annual commemoration in Lower Manhattan of this horrible day.[71] Union activists, alongside the descendants of the victims of the 1911 fire, honor the names of the Triangle victims. This memorial event has also served as a solemn occasion to remember all of the lives of workers lost during the previous year. In the years before the COVID pandemic, it was the plight of New York City's undocumented construction workers who died or were seriously injured at non-union worksites which were spotlighted.

These gatherings have helped to highlight — with the decline of the union movement — just how dramatic an increase we have seen in the precarity of employment itself. In recent years, they have also referenced the dozens of undocumented immigrants that have died at non-union construction worksites, without basic protections of represented employees — like workers' compensation, disability, and death benefits.

In 2021, the Triangle Fire Coalition and the New York Central Labor Council of the AFL-CIO produced a virtual celebration on the anniversary to highlight the plight of the nation's millions of essential workers and their families who have been infected with COVID-19 and the thousands who have died from the deadly virus. As with the death of the Triangle workers, the culpability for the death toll is to be found at the confluence of the willful disregard by corporations and the government of the spread of the highly contagious and deadly virus, at the beginning of the pandemic, in places like the nation's meat-processing plants. It was there that the Trump administration, in complete supplication to the meat producers, subverted the efforts of unions and local public health officials to stop the spread of the virus.

Indeed, since the onset of the virus, thousands of workers have suffered nationwide due to a lack of adequate workplace protections during the pandemic. In nearly all cases, having union representation could have helped.

Consequently, pandemic-related labor strife has been sparked all around the country. In Amazon's Bessemer, Alabama, distribution plant, the multinational behemoth did all it could to defeat the union organizing drive of 6,000 mostly Black workers into the Retail, Wholesale and Department Store Union (RWDSU).[72]

March 22, at a March Moral Monday celebration before the April vote, Reverend Dr. William Barber took Amazon's CEO, Jeff Bezos, to task for trying to use his commitment of gifting $10 million to African American causes "to show he is concerned about Black Lives Matter," while seeking to derail Amazon workers' bid for collective bargaining. Barber is the co-leader of the national Poor People's Campaign, which was originally launched at the SCLC Conference of November of 1967.

"I am going to say today that Amazon doesn't care about Black lives, if you give chump change to Black organizations but then block the labor and union rights for workers right here in Bessemer," Barber preached. "Don't play with us like that. If there are any national organizations taking money from Jeff Bezos, they ought to give it back until he stops the attack on these workers."

During the pandemic, at least 20,000 Amazon workers fell sick with COVID-19, some of whom died. In contrast, Bezos's personal wealth "skyrocketed from $113 billion to $189 billion during COVID," Barber said. He observed that spike in wealth happened while eight million more Americans fell into poverty during the pandemic, which also continues to pose significant occupational health risks for essential workers that are not getting hazard pay.

Amazon's labor pains extended to New York State as well. In February 2021, New York State Attorney General Letitia James sued Amazon for "repeatedly and persistently" failing "to comply with its obligation to institute reasonable and adequate measures to protect its workers from the spread of the virus in its New York City facilities" in Staten Island and in Queens.[73] Attorney General James alleged that Amazon's "flagrant disregard for health and safety requirements...threatened serious illness and grave harm to the thousands of workers in these facilities" and posed a "continued substantial and specific danger to the public health." James also called out the company for allegedly retaliating against its employees who had raised concerns about how Amazon was addressing the considerable occupational health challenges posed by the pandemic.

According to RWDSU, Amazon's tactics were taken to a new level in the multinational's successful drive to defeat the organizing vote in Alabama. "We won't let Amazon's lies, deception, and illegal activities go unchallenged, which is why we are formally filing charges against all of the egregious and blatantly illegal actions taken by Amazon during the union vote," wrote RWDSU President Stuart Applebaum after the tally was announced. "Amazon knew full well that, unless they did everything they possibly could — even illegal activity — their workers would have continued supporting the union."

He continued, "That's why they required all their employees to attend lecture after lecture, filled with mistruths and lies, where workers had to listen to the company demand they oppose the union. That's why they flooded the internet, the airwaves and social media with ads spreading misinformation. That's why they brought in dozens of outsiders and union-busters to walk the floor of the warehouse. That's why they bombarded people with signs throughout the facility and with text messages and calls at home. And that's why they have been lying about union dues in a right-to-work state. Amazon's conduct has been despicable."

Yet even as the union movement was dealt a setback in Alabama, a dynamic coalition of immigrant community groups and labor unions was winning unprecedented victories in New York State. In addition to successfully lobbying to raise taxes on the state's wealthiest individuals and corporations by $4.6 billion, they convinced the legislature to pass the nation's first unemployment compensation program to provide $2.1 billion for undocumented workers.

Just two weeks later, the same coalition won passage in Albany of the NY HERO Act. The bill creates workplace standards to prevent the spread of airborne viruses and mandates that even non-union employers create workplace-safety committees to protect their employees. "Every day, working people have gone above-and-beyond to carry us through the pandemic and, for too many of them, the cost has been their own health and even death," wrote Mario Cilento, president of the New York State AFL-CIO. "The least we can do as a state is help ensure that their employers take every reasonable measure necessary to keep them safe on the job."

He continued, "This pandemic has exposed the weaknesses in workplace safety. The NY HERO Act changes that, by ensuring workers have a safe working environment now and, just as important, for future communicable-disease events." The measure is believed to be one of the most comprehensive in the nation for the private sector. It requires the provision of safety standards and personal protective equipment, as well as adequate ventilation and social-distancing requirements.

According to the New York Committee for Occupational Safety and Health ("NYCOSH"), a non-profit union-supported advocacy group, at least 250,000 essential workers in New York contracted symptomatic COVID, and another 150,000 experienced an asymptomatic infection, which health experts say could lead to still unknown health consequences. With more than 30 million Americans infected by COVID-19, we can project — depending on the research study one examines — that as many as one in three Americans will be left with lingering health effects from COVID of varying severity. That is millions of people, many of whom will have contracted the virus while working. Yet, as of now, most states do not provide a Workers' Compensation presumption from COVID — meaning that employers can fight the claims by disabled workers, and many already have.[74]

One of the challenges for the pandemic-inspired labor movement is that no one really knows how many workers have died or been infected on the job. We have hints here and there from reporting projects. For example, thanks to a joint reporting project by *The Guardian* and *Kaiser Health News*, we do know that more than 3,500 healthcare workers who were under 60 years of age died from COVID, with 700 of them from just New York and New Jersey.[75] We also know that hundreds of law enforcement officers have died from COVID-19, making it the leading cause of death for that workforce.[76]

Certainly, though, the COVID infection and death toll for healthcare workers and first responders is only a partial picture of the bigger picture of the occupational health crisis that has ensnared the entire essential workforce. Some legislators are working to change that. New York State Senator Brad Hoylman lives in Lower Manhattan, just three blocks away from the site of the Triangle Fire and not far from the World Trade Center (WTC). Recently, Hoylman has introduced state legislation to create a voluntary COVID Health Registry, similar to the one that was created for the 9/11 WTC first responders and survivors. It was the WTC Registry that helped both state and federal policymakers gauge the public health implications from the toxic exposure of that crisis as they only became evident years later.

"We don't know what the long-term effects of COVID are yet," Hoylman said. "Yet we know there are lingering side effects, from

74

respiratory conditions to psychotic breakdowns, and that is all just coming to light. Hopefully, this is not a lifetime disability, but there are some worrisome signs that suggest the impact could be long-term for as many as 10 percent or more of COVID cases." New York State is one of at least 30 states that do not have a workers' compensation guarantee for essential workers who contracted the deadly virus at work. In these states, workers that are sidelined can be left unemployed without the financial resources to support themselves while they convalesce.

Similarly difficult to account for are the impacts on undocumented workers, many of whom kept working amid the pandemic. "I am hopeful that this kind of evidence of long-term health consequences from COVID [collected in the health registry] can help change that," Hoylman said. Without these basic numbers, the number of essential workers battling COVID-19 will remain hidden. The best way to honor the essential workers that have died from COVID is to honor the ones that are still living. We can most effectively structure the occupational health protections for the next pandemic by tracking the effects in the wake of this virus.

Only disciplined and passionate organizing can make sure the essential workers who have already given so much remain visible in a country where market forces have so consistently disregarded what is inconvenient to acknowledge and address.

Chapter 6: Squeezing Out Essential Investments

How we choose to spend the money the nation raises collectively through taxation is a reflection of our collective values. It is how we actualize what it is we want our country to be — not just in the moment, but decades into the future.

One of the most obvious, yet least discussed, ways we manifest our national "stuck-ness" is the hugely disproportionate share of our discretionary federal spending that goes to the Pentagon year after year, decade after decade.

We remain a "Stuck Nation," in large measure, because of a bipartisan consensus in Washington that, whatever other challenges we face in terms of public health or climate change, we must maintain obscene levels of military spending — even if we have to borrow hundreds of billions of dollars to do it. The two political parties in Congress still can't agree on the outcome of the 2020 election; but a critical mass of members of both parties continue to back higher military spending, often rationalizing it as critical support for local employers. What gets no attention are the tangible and mounting lost-opportunity costs that come from underfunding early childhood education and public health, while at the same time deferring basic infrastructure upgrades and investments in water supply projects, healthcare facilities and transportation networks.

The National Priorities Project (NPP) describes itself as "the only nonprofit, non-partisan federal budget research organization in the nation with the mission to make the federal budget accessible to the American public."[77] According to NPP, our military spending — approaching three quarters of a trillion dollars annually — is greater than 10 of the next big "defense spenders" combined — which includes China, Russia, Saudi Arabia, the United Kingdom, France, Japan, Germany, India, South Africa, and Brazil. Twenty years after 9/11, our $750 billion in annual Pentagon spending accounts for 53 percent of the federal government's discretionary spending. As NPP reports, "For the first time in a long time, the president's discretionary budget would provide as much funding for domestic priorities as the Pentagon and war. But…every other priority is a small fraction of the Pentagon budget. Case in point: the CDC budget, which for obvious reasons should be considered a critical part of our national security spending (if you take those words at their dictionary meanings). The Biden proposal calls for an increase to the CDC budget. But, *the proposed increase in the Pentagon budget is bigger than the entire proposed CDC discretionary budget.*"[78]

NPP continues, "The Biden proposal does a lot right, in calling for increases to domestic spending priorities that have been underfunded for years. But it's stuck in an outdated version of what national security means, revving up the Pentagon budget at the very time when we need to be shifting funding to security based on clean energy, public health, and racial and economic equality." While President Biden was the progressive alternative to Trump, there's been a depressing continuity with the White House's increasing military spending.

There's a direct link between the oversized military spending, which is done by increasing our national debt, and the squeezing out of other essential investments in the American people and a wounded world. According to the Center for Responsive Politics, the top 10 defense-industry donors gave more than $30 million to congressional campaigns and political-action committees in the 2019-20 cycle.[79] But that's just a rounding error in the $1 billion in dark money spent in our politics since the Supreme Court's controversial 5-to-4 decision in 2010, in the *Citizens United* case, reversing long-standing campaign finance restrictions and holding that any restrictions on "independent political spending" by corporations violated their First Amendment right to free speech.[80]

As noted in a research report by the Brennan Center for Justice,[81] "The ruling has ushered in massive increases in political spending from outside groups, dramatically expanding the already outsized political influence of wealthy donors, corporations, and special interest groups.... In the immediate aftermath of the *Citizens United* decision, analysts focused much of their attention on how the Supreme Court designated corporate spending on elections as free speech. But perhaps the most significant outcomes of *Citizens United* have been the creation of super PACs [political action committees], which empower the wealthiest donors, and the expansion of dark money through shadowy nonprofits that don't disclose their donors."[82]

In Senator Sheldon Whitehouse's 2017 book *CAPTURED: The Corporate Infiltration of American Democracy*, the author explained how, in the 2016 election cycle, these same shadowy corporate interests successfully targeted for defeat three US Senate candidates, including campaign finance-reform champion Senator Russ Feingold.[83] "This is happening mostly behind the scenes," wrote Whitehouse. "All the public sees is a Congress that won't even consider climate change, or fair pharmaceutical pricing, or banning dark money, or investigating whatever financial ties our president [Trump] has to foreign interests, but that will pass sleazy midnight tax bills that pour money to big political donors." He continued, "Think I'm kidding? The recent Republican 'donor rewards program' tax bill added $1.5 trillion to our national debt and showered the bulk of it on wealthy corporate interests of the sort most likely behind those hundreds of millions in dark money. That's a big payback." Whitehouse shares the rate of return for mega-donor Sheldon Adelson, who got a $700 million windfall from the Trump GOP tax bill after spreading around $30 million in political spending, and a Texas oil refiner who spent $1.5 million to influence decision-makers and got a $1.9 billion tax windfall.

As a consequence of how *Citizens United* facilitated the inundation of our politics with dark money, there isn't any realm of regulation or government spending that has not been tainted by its undue influence. Agenda items in the public interest — like maintaining a robust public health system — get sidelined by the pay-to-play nature of our politics. In the oversight and regulation of healthcare, the profitability of the insurance companies, big pharma and the for-profit healthcare systems set the agenda.

The country is still in the midst of a once-in-a-century, mass-death event and a meltdown of our healthcare system. There's been much public hand-wringing about how the nation's poor communities of color were disproportionately hit by COVID; and, even now, those areas still suffer from long-standing healthcare disparities due to chronic underinvestment. Between 1975 and 2019, the United States saw the closure of close to 1,100 hospitals, particularly in our poorest rural and urban communities. This massive retrenchment contributed to the pre-existing conditions that resulted in the catastrophic failure of our basic public health infrastructure in so many communities during the COVID pandemic.

Trump tried to downplay the severity of the public health crisis — and the federal government's accountability for addressing it — seeking to gain political leverage by playing states and regions of the nation off against each other. It was a divide-and-conquer strategy, which Trump hoped to use to hold on to power despite his failure to lead the country out of the pandemic. Even as COVID continued to ravage the country in the waning months of Trump's tenure, he focused on holding on to power by undermining the legitimacy of the election he'd lost. Rather than ensuring an orderly transition and following through on delivering the vaccine program that would set the country on a course toward recovery, he focused all of his attention on inciting an unprecedented violent insurrection.

During that January 6th attack, the angry Trump mob stormed the Capitol and, in the process, killed Capitol Police Officer Brian Sicknick, who was also a veteran of our never-ending "war on terror" overseas.[84] As a civilian — back home in New Jersey after his service in the Middle East — in 2004, he had written a letter to his local newspaper, in support of Senator John Kerry for president over President George W. Bush, observing that US foreign policy was itself "one reason the world has become as dangerous as it is." In another letter to his local paper, he had pleaded for his fellow

Americans to pay some attention to what was happening with the country's military that "was stretched very thin" and whose morale had become "dangerously low."

The violent assault on the US Capitol during our democracy's most vulnerable time — the peaceful transition of power — resulted in five deaths and serious injury to dozens of responding police officers. Even months later, Congressional and Senate Republicans — whose own physical security had been threatened that day — were still too afraid of former President Trump and his supporters to support bipartisan legislation convening a 9/11-style commission to investigate how a nation, which had spent trillions to fight terror abroad, was so vulnerable to a mob of mostly white domestic terrorists here at home. That vote could not get sufficient support from Republican Senators, despite the personal lobbying from Sicknick's mother, Gladys, and his life partner, Sandra Gardner, who traveled to Washington to plead their case for the review of the attack.

In the months since, prosecutors have identified active-duty law enforcement officers, as well as retired members of the US military, as participants in the insurrection. To this day, dozens of members of Congress persist in subscribing to Trump's "Big Lie" that the 2020 election was stolen from him. "The fact that, in running for a second term, Trump won 74 million votes is an absolutely astonishing fact that has gotten too little attention," said Andrew Bacevich, a noted historian, West Point graduate, and retired US Army Colonel. His service spanned from Vietnam to the Gulf War. "It is not simply that some soldiers are alienated, or police officers are alienated. We have got about half the country that's angry and alienated."

Bacevich believes the Nixon-era decision to go with an all-voluntary military, to end the draft that had encountered major resistance during the Vietnam War, has led to a dangerous "gap between the armed forces and American society." He said, "I think the adverse consequences of that gap are pretty obvious and sadly ignored.... And the most important consequence is that the American people are not particularly invested in what the American military is doing, where it is doing it, and what effects and with what consequences.... I think this has allowed the government — quite frankly a militarized

81

government — to wage endless wars, a list of campaigns, many small and brief middle-sized and protracted. What has that produced? An incredible amount of waste — wasted money, wasted lives, broken lives — with precious little to show for it by way of a positive return."

The disconnect between the Pentagon's post-9/11, further-notice war footing and the direction of the rest of the country was on full display after members of the US Senate Armed Services Committee, including Senators Lindsey Graham and John McCain, had to admit in 2017 — after four US soldiers died in Niger — that they were unaware that American troops were even deployed in that African country. And far from a "positive return," this further-notice war footing helped collapse countries, pollute the environment, accelerate global warming, and set into motion the largest refugee migration since the Second World War.

Since 9/11 alone, 7,000 of our soldiers have died, and well over 50,000 have been injured. According to the Cost of War Project at Brown University's Watson Institute for International and Public Affairs, close to 340,000 civilians have been killed in the crossfire and over 20 million have been made refugees.[85] As the Biden administration plans to leave Afghanistan, it's estimated we have spent almost $6.5 trillion in borrowed money and, in the process, helped proliferate terrorist groups.

Consider the lost-opportunity costs incurred while we set out to scour the world for terrorists. We let our nation's infrastructure fall into total disrepair, buried our kids in hundreds of billions of dollars in higher-education debt, and closed rural and urban hospitals — all while keeping the federal minimum wage at a scandalous $7.25 an hour. This is how you create a "Stuck Nation": funding with trillions a military machine, while ignoring climate change, shortchanging healthcare, education, and housing, as well as the basic physical infrastructure upon which civil society depends. At the same time, increasingly shifting wealth and income to an increasingly small percentage of the population, and simultaneously convening at Davos to ponder why regular people just can't get ahead.

Aside from what we hear from public intellectuals, like Cornel West, these connections between our addiction to militarism and the human priorities we neglect are rarely contextualized. As the

Republicans gathered in Cleveland to nominate Donald Trump in 2016, I left the convention to attend a public-policy and social-action forum, "IMPACT," at Mount Olivet Institutional Baptist Church, one of the city's largest African American congregations. Cornel West was the keynote speaker. Before his speech, I interviewed him in the choir loft: [86]

ROBERT HENNELLY: We know there are 6,000 zombie homes in Cleveland.[87] Fifty percent of Cleveland's children are living in poverty. In Philadelphia, there are 40,000 vacant lots and homes. In the last eight years, we've seen the largest loss of African-American household wealth in the history of the republic. Why is that not emerging as a central issue of the presidential campaign?

CORNEL WEST: Well, it's just very difficult to shatter the neoliberal hegemony in the public conversation. The neoliberal ideology comes in a number of different colors. It could be Bill Clinton, it could be Barack Obama, it could be Hillary Clinton. And that neoliberal hegemony means that trying to raise the issues of poverty — not just Black poverty, but poverty across the board, to really zero-in on Wall Street domination of Congress, to really zero-in on corporate power, to really zero-in on the military industrial complex — that's a difficult thing. Neoliberal press, neoliberal politicians — it's hard to get fellow citizens to look at the world through a very different lens as opposed to a neoliberal lens.

RH: It seems we've had this metaphor we're stuck in for decades now of a war on poverty, and there seems to be more poverty. War on drugs, more drugs. War on terror, more terror.

CW: More terror, that's true.

RH: You're one of the few public intellectuals who are linking the economic expenditure for war with these other public ills. Why aren't we discussing the collateral damage of this never-ending war?

CW: Of course, the first thing to keep in mind is that we don't even expose precious fellow citizens [members of the military] to the

83

bodies of soldiers who are killed in Afghanistan and other places. So you already have a hiding and concealing of the realities of war. We've been at war for over 14 years, 15 years, in Afghanistan.

Then you've got 54 percent of the budget as a whole going to military expenditures, and a lot of that actually is not fully accounted for because there are certain unlimited expenditures when it comes to the Pentagon, but no serious discussion about that. There is a consensus, Democrats and Republicans, Obama and [Senate Majority Leader] Mitch McConnell, on this dominance of military expenditure, and [that] makes it very difficult.

When Dr. King said the bombs that dropped in Vietnam also landed in ghettos, he didn't just mean Black ghettos — he meant brown barrios, he meant white brothers and sisters in Appalachia, indigenous brothers and sisters on the reservations. There's just no money [for social investment].

So, we're in a logjam. That's what neoliberalism does. It's a logjam when you allow for corporate power on the one hand, military industrial complex on the other hand, and then think to be progressive is only talk about social issues.

RH: One of the things you seem to be in touch with is that since 2008, for working people, the economic situation has continued to unravel.

CW: Absolutely.

RH: According to the National Association of Counties, out of 3,069 counties, only 7 percent have recovered, by their measurement.[88] So, in other words, we are not really seeing our social circumstance reflected in our media, which leaves us in isolation. What's a consequence of that, politically and spiritually?

CW: Well, I think the first point to keep in mind is that through a neoliberal lens, recovery is measured by how well the stock market is doing, and how well corporate profits are doing. And they have been doing very well. I just [look at] the QE2 — the quantitative easing — coming out of the Federal Reserve…because that's the benchmark.[89]

It's not what is the quality of life of everyday people, of working people. And as you rightly say, there has been no recovery there, not in the real economy. In the stock market, indeed. So, you miss the social misery that's out there, and of course, [the presidential candidacy of] Donald Trump is part of the backlash. He is part of the deeply right-wing populist backlash because so many of white working-class brothers and sisters, but especially the brothers, are hurting, and that hurt is real. But unfortunately it's not geared toward accountability toward elites at the top; it's scapegoating the most vulnerable on the bottom.

RH: If we pull back a bit, we know that our young people, 16- to 24-year-olds, have a crisis. In New York City, 30 percent of Black men between the ages of 20-24 are not working and they're not in school.[90] Globally, the figure is 50 percent — 7 million in Mexico alone. At some point, don't we have to call into question the social obligation of capital to employ this generation? And how do we do that?

CW: The good news is that there is a magnificent moral, spiritual, and political awakening taking place among the younger generation in the midst of the American empire. The Bernie Sanders campaign was a great example of young folk comin' alive, becoming involved.

What is it now, 58 percent of young people across race and class say socialism is preferable over capitalism? Why? Because what they have lived has been more and more the underside of capitalist order, which is one of massive unemployment, decrepit education, unbelievable student debt. But also, spiritually — it's a dog-eat-dog world, obsessed with the 11th Commandment: "Thou shalt not get caught." That way of being in the world is being called into question among the younger generation. And in that sense, there's tremendous signs of hope."

Since that interview, we have had a pandemic and a right-wing insurrection, while the costs of our overspending on the military and underinvesting in everything else — like healthcare — have continued to mount.

According to a May 2021 report by the U.S. Government Accountability Office (GAO) — a nonpartisan research agency—our country is in the midst of nothing short of a mental-health meltdown.[91] Years of neglect and disinvestment have resulted in a massive shortage of inpatient psychiatric beds, outpatient programs, and the trained professionals that both require. The GAO noted that, the year before the pandemic, an "estimated 52 million adults in the United States (21 percent) were reported to have a mental, behavioral, or emotional disorder." GAO's analysis continued. "Additionally, 20 million people aged 12 or older had a substance use disorder (either an alcohol use disorder, an illicit drug use disorder, or both). Experts have expressed concerns that the incidence of behavioral health conditions would increase as a result of stressors associated with the COVID-19 pandemic — such as social isolation and job loss — and, in November 2020, we reported early evidence of increases in these conditions linked to the pandemic…. For example, results of CDC Household Pulse surveys, conducted from April 2020 through February 2021, found that the percentage of adults reporting symptoms of anxiety or depression averaged 38.1 across 24 separate survey collection periods — ranging from a low of 33.9 in mid-May to a high of 42.6 in mid-November," GAO found. "In comparison, a CDC survey conducted in 2019, using similar questions, found that about 11.0 percent of U.S. adults reported experiencing these symptoms from January to June 2019. Recent data also show that overdose deaths and suicide attempts have increased during the pandemic."

In September 2020, the Substance Abuse and Mental Health Services Administration ("SAMHSA") reported opioid deaths in some regions of the country were as much as 25 to 50 percent higher during the pandemic than the comparison time period in 2019. "An analysis of CDC data published in February 2021 found that the share of emergency department visits for suicide attempts and drug overdoses were 26 and 36 percent higher, respectively, for the period of mid-March through mid-October 2020 compared to the same time period in 2019." The GAO cites a February 2021 survey by the National Council for Behavioral Health, noting that its members reduced staff during the pandemic and "decreased services, with 27 percent of member organizations reported laying off employees; 45 percent reported closing some programs; 23 percent furloughed employees; 35 percent decreased the hours for staff; and 68 percent reported having to cancel, reschedule, or turn away patients in the last 3 months."

No doubt, the conventional infrastructure debate between the Biden White House and Congressional Republicans is too often focused on the quality of the roads in and out of the gated communities of the rich and powerful. But to get the rest of the nation unstuck — where most of us live — we need to radically reset how we define "infrastructure." It must include the overlooked communities hardest hit by the pandemic. Rest assured, those are the very same places most likely to be hit the hardest in the next pandemic.

A pandemic can be similar to a war, when calculating its human toll. The most precise way public health researchers can get a handle on the impact of something like COVID-19 is to compare the number of total deaths recorded in a specific place during the pandemic with death tallies from prior years. That analysis will yield a figure known as "excess deaths" — which simply means deaths above and beyond what would normally be expected. That figure captures not just COVID-19 deaths, but also the number of people who were unable to access healthcare at a moment in their lives when a chronic condition was becoming life-threatening. It also includes individuals whose primary cause of death may have been something else, but who were also infected with COVID-19. And now that the dust has settled and the data are being tabulated, America's excess death numbers over the past year are staggering.

The importance of tabulating such a dark statistic is twofold: Its record-breaking nature is due both to our largely for-profit healthcare system and to government incompetence. Indeed, for decades our government ignored the warnings from public health experts that the country was not properly prepared for the pandemic we have experienced. It's not like no one could have seen the pandemic coming. In his book, *The Great Influenza,*_first published in 2004, John M. Barry presaged the COVID-19 crisis, describing how "hospitals, like every other industry, have gotten more efficient by cutting costs, which means virtually no excess capacity — on a per capita basis, the United States has far fewer hospital beds than a few decades ago."[92]

He continued. "Indeed, during a routine influenza season, usage of respirators rises to nearly 100 percent; in a pandemic, most people who needed a mechanical respirator would not get one."[93] As we have learned firsthand over the last year, because the healthcare system was overwhelmed,[94] getting accurate cause-of-death data was itself a work in progress.[95] No doubt, huge numbers of COVID-19 cases may have been missed. In other instances, individuals may have died at home or succumbed to a chronic illness that was written off as COVID when it was not.[96]

The one constant, comparative data point is death itself, from any and all causes. Like births, deaths are something we track with some precision. So, one way that medical researchers can get a sense of the scale of the impact of something like COVID is to compare the total number of deaths from all causes during the pandemic and compare it with the same data point over several prior years. Such an "excess death" analysis will capture the collateral impact of overwhelmed healthcare systems that were under-resourced long before the pandemic. It will include the people that died as a consequence of opting not to go to the hospital for an unrelated condition for fear of catching COVID-19. While that might not count as a COVID-19 death *per se*, it tells us something about what happens when we permit healthcare to operate without any margin or redundancy — what is effectively a form of rationing healthcare.

According to a recently published study in the *Journal of the American Medical Association*, which looked at the rate of excess deaths from March 1, 2020, to January 2, 2021, there were 522,368 "excess deaths," contrasted against averages over the same period from 2014 to 2019.[97] At the start of 2021, COVID-19 deaths were reported at just over 350,186. By comparing the "excess rate" of death with the COVID-19 reported data, linked to its location, we can get some sense of where the public health system had the hardest time holding up under the once-in-a-century strain of a mass-death event. The study, published by researchers with the Virginia Commonwealth University School of Medicine and the Yale School of Public Health, calculated that COVID-19 accounted for 72.4 percent of the excess mortality. The balance may have been "either immediate or delayed mortality from undocumented COVID-19 infection, or non-COVID-19 deaths secondary to the pandemic, such as from delayed care or behavioral health crises." While nationally there was a 23 percent increase in excess mortality during the pandemic, New York State, which lost close to 50,000 to COVID, saw the nation's highest spike, with a 38 percent jump in excess deaths — though Mississippi and New Jersey actually exceeded New York State on a *per capita* basis, according to the researchers.

In an editorial that was published with the study, Dr. Alan M. Garber wrote of the importance of grasping the bigger picture, beyond the daily COVID dashboard.[98] "There is no more visible or alarming manifestation of the toll of the COVID-19 pandemic than the deaths it has caused," he noted. "The missteps in responding to an outbreak that not only could be, but largely was, predicted should not give governments confidence that they are prepared for threats that are more speculative and possibly further in the future," Garber continued. "Failure to anticipate the scale of the potential damage from such future catastrophes will only exacerbate the tendency to downplay their importance, making it less likely that governments will prepare adequately. That is why understanding the toll of a pandemic is an important step in the right direction."

In New York City, where COVID killed more than 32,000 city residents, fighting the virus inspired life-saving innovations. According to Dr. Mitch Katz, the CEO of New York City Health + Hospitals (NYC H+H), it also exposed long-standing healthcare disparities that left some neighborhoods more at the mercy of the highly contagious and deadly virus. NYC H+H, the nation's largest municipal hospital system, includes 11 hospitals and saw some of the highest patient death counts early on. Over the course of the pandemic, thousands of H+H workers from a myriad of job titles were sidelined by the deadly virus, which took the lives of 53 employees.

It was in the throes of this nearly unprecedented public health emergency that NYC H+H found ways to improve patient care, while at the same time reducing the exposure of staff to the deadly virus which helped to slow the spread of the virus. "We have done a lot of work from the first wave about putting glass doors in or glass in the walls to create a window for cameras in the patient rooms, microphones so that patients can be monitored safely, without going into the room…and that is a positive development, whether there's COVID or some other infectious disease," Dr. Katz said. "So, I think we learned how to make our hospitals safer for the care of patients with infectious diseases."

For Dr. Katz, one of the most sobering discoveries was how pre-existing disparities in the city's private and public hospital infrastructure left some communities so much more vulnerable during the pandemic. "I think the fact that we had so many fewer hospital beds in Queens, compared to Manhattan, was one of the stark lessons," he said. "That's part of why it was so much more challenging to deal with the pandemic in Queens and Elmhurst Hospitals, because there were so few beds, considering the size of the population in Queens compared to Manhattan and other parts of New York State. The discrepancy in the number of beds, I'd say, was an issue."

Dr. Katz had established a national reputation, leading the public hospital systems in San Francisco and Los Angeles before returning home to New York. After years of experience on the frontlines of urban healthcare on both coasts, he believes that the nation's vulnerability to COVID-19 can be traced back to a steady disinvestment in public health that started during the Reagan era. "Yes, the pandemic shows how we have to build up our public health infrastructure, so that we are better prepared for what people need," he said. As the city, state, and federal governments all attempt to regroup after more than a half-million deaths and the infection of well over 30 million, Dr. Katz believes policy-makers would be well-advised to consult the data, not just on COVID deaths *per se*, but on excess mortality rates by neighborhoods. "I think we have some sense already of the excess mortality that occurred among people who had COVID and didn't come forward for testing," he said. "Some of those people were undocumented immigrants or people who were very low income and feared coming forward to a hospital…. Some of that excess mortality we know were people who were having heart attacks or other serious health conditions and didn't come forward for care, because they were so frightened of catching COVID from the hospital. So, I think the excess mortality is very helpful. Frankly it doesn't have to be exact. We can all acknowledge there were a number of people who died and didn't have a COVID test. It's the general population trend that matters."

Yet, despite 600,000 Americans dying from COVID and another 33 million infections from the deadly disease, we continue to ignore the connections between US militarism and the nation's chronic underinvestment in public health that left the nation so vulnerable to the virus. As we sink hundreds of billions deeper into debt to maintain weapons systems that we hope not to use, we ignore or defer the investments required to reduce the risk of climate events that cause a massive loss of life and property, like Hurricane Sandy. These events have been occurring with increasing frequency as the climate crisis accelerates.

Like the pandemic, predicted by public health journalists like Laurie Garrett, these traumatic climate events are entirely foreseeable. Yet, the forces of greed that dominate our politics resist spending the resources to anticipate either kind of catastrophic event; because wealth accumulation is their controlling imperative. When you look at which communities are the most vulnerable to climate-change events, they are often the very same ones most ravaged by COVID.

If America is to get well, which is the first step to escaping the undertow of this pandemic and preparing for staving off the next, we have to uplift these places where regular access to quality healthcare was a socio-economic, pre-existing condition that helped drive the local body count. Our own individual health is linked to the health of our neighbors. That's not scripture. That's biology.

The only remedy is the power that resides in each one of us, acting collectively in our mutual self-interest, to advocate for these places, wherever we live.

Chapter 7: Dismantling Organized Protections

There's no better example of America's disregard for working people (of all colors) than the 2018 federal government shutdown caused by President Trump's maniacal pursuit of a multibillion-dollar wall on the border with Mexico that he had claimed, during his 2016 campaign, would be paid for by our neighbor to the south.

That shutdown started just before Christmas and extended for 35 days, leaving 800,000 federal workers — many of them people of color — without a paycheck. And yet, because of the nature of their work in job titles including corrections officer, nurse, and air traffic controller, half of them had to continue to work for those 35 days without compensation.

In so many ways, this brutal maneuver by Trump was a foreshadowing of his ignoring the risk of COVID, which would claim the lives of tens of thousands of first responders, healthcare workers, transportation personnel, and the rest of the face-to-face essential workforce — including federal civil servants who could not work from home.

In January 2019, the National Treasury Employees Union (NTEU), which represents 150,000 federal workers, sued the Trump administration on behalf of Customs and Border Protection Officers Eleazar Avalos and James Davis, and the many of thousands of essential workers like them, alleging that compelling their uncompensated labor violated the federal Fair Labor Standards Act. According to *The Washington Post*,[99] their average salary was around

$85,600 a year, but almost 111,000 of them make less than $50,000, with thousands of TSA agents making $30,000 a year.[100] The fact that 40 percent of them were veterans just added to the injustice and indignity.

Trump had come into office pledging to dismantle the federal government and had gone about doing it with a blunt instrument.

Outside a federal building in Lower Manhattan on a bitter cold Martin Luther King Day in January 2019, scores of workers with the American Federation of Government Employees (AFGE) and NTEU tried to stay warm while blowing off steam as they expressed their frustration. "It is an abomination when 800,000 people are told by their president they are so worthless they don't deserve a paycheck for a day's wage," AFGE organizer Gabriel Pedreira told the crowd.

Mr. Pedreira, noting it was Martin Luther King Jr.'s birthday, invoked the slain Civil-Rights leader's record of supporting organized labor and public workers. "It's important to remember his views on labor and that all labor has dignity," he said. "Now, when you send people to work and tell them they are not entitled to a paycheck, you take away their dignity. That's what you do. You say they are not equal to other workers — they are less than other workers."

Rev. Stephan Marshall of the National Action Network told the gathering, "I just want to make it clear that when you have heard reports of 800,000 workers who are locked out without being paid, I come to you today to shine a light on hundreds of thousands or more that are attached to that one paycheck — we have millions of children, single mothers, single fathers who are being hijacked, held hostage by this President."

At a union rally in Pittsburgh, workers made their case to the local media. "We have members across the state who are worried about feeding their families and paying their bills," said AFGE Local 332 President William Reese. "The stress level is at an all-time high, but despite these current hardships our folks continue to serve the flying public and carry out their vital mission."

Across the country, federal workers held press briefings and rallies to rouse public opposition to the shutdown, while soup kitchens and food pantries scrambled to meet the heightened needs.

Richard Wolff, Professor Emeritus of the Department of Economics at the University of Massachusetts Amherst, noted that in any other Western democracy such an affront to working people would have been met by a general strike. "There's no question in my mind you would have had a general strike," Wolff said. "The first thing that goes is all transportation. I know France best, and what happens is all the trains stop, buses, airlines, everything stops. And sometimes they add the utilities, the gas and telephone. And almost always the government caves."

Wolff says that organized labor in Europe can press their case, "because the mass of the population sympathizes [with the workers], and the unions have done their homework and they have shown the mass of the people to see it their way. The French unions would say they [the government] are requiring us to work without pay. And that's it. The conversation is over at that point, because the population would find it so outrageous."

Tragically, American corporate news media couldn't fully appreciate Trump's shutdown as a "tell" of his intended dismantling. Perhaps to see it for what it was would have meant facing their own complicity in his rise to power. The free media coverage they had given him in his run-up to the 2016 election had been part of their Faustian bargain for ever more clicks, listeners, and viewers.

Long before the shutdown, Trump and his cabal, led by experienced Beltway hands — like former South Carolina Congressman Mick Mulvaney, who served as both the director of the Office of Management and Budget as well as Trump's acting White House Chief of Staff — went about the business of trying to actually dismantle the federal government. That dismantling, years before the COVID crisis, proved to be part of the inefficacy of Trump's response to the pandemic.

However, having former corporate executives run the regulatory agencies that oversaw their industry or having former White House officials and members of Congress go to work for those industries was a long-established custom before Trump got to the White House. For decades, under both Democratic and Republican administrations, the federal government had developed a regulatory structure in its agencies that included a critical mass of career civil-service scientists who kept the agencies running (and acted as an ongoing check on the excesses of big energy and big pharma), despite the bipartisan revolving doors at the tops of the agencies.

What Trump's wrecking crew had in mind was something entirely new. By directly attacking the ranks of the civil service with a full-court press to drive out the federal unions and eliminate the post-Watergate reforms — including the network of inspectors general — Trump laid the groundwork for being able to subvert even the U.S. Centers for Disease Control and Prevention (CDC). From even before Trump had been sworn in, his junta had taken aim at the system of inspectors general. They hit the ground running by making calls to several inspectors general telling them they needed to resign or face being fired. After strongly negative congressional pushback, the Trump administration backed off their efforts at a purge.

Congress, hoping to increase the public's confidence in government integrity in the aftermath of the Watergate scandal 45 years ago, had passed the Inspector General Act of 1978. It was designed to provide independent oversight and public accountability for 12 of the major agencies in the executive branch — including the Central Intelligence Agency, the Department of Defense, the Environmental Protection Agency, and the Federal Elections Commission, among others. Today, there are 73 Offices of Inspector General (OIG) with 14,000 employees.

Department of Justice IG Michael Horowitz, who chaired the Council of Inspectors General on Integrity and Efficiency (CIGIE), testified before a 2017 House Oversight Committee hearing that the threatening calls from the transition team left all of the inspectors general, whether they were called or not, "concerned about not just their own positions but about the institution [of Inspector General] itself." Inspectors general are charged with providing Congress with independent audits and detailed reports on their respective agencies' activities and offering federal employees confidential tip lines to report instances of waste, fraud, or other potential abuse without fear of reprisal.

More than halfway through President Trump's term in office, a dozen IG posts either remained vacant or were being held down by individuals in an "acting" capacity.

Good-government groups were particularly alarmed about comments that Mr. Trump made at a January 2, 2019, Cabinet meeting where, with reporters present, he expressed open hostility to the role of inspectors general and described their fact-finding and subsequent public-disclosure processes as "insane."

In a letter to Defense Secretary Patrick Shanahan, Danielle Brian, the Executive Director of the Project on Government Oversight — a good-government group — wrote of being particularly "disturbed" that Trump spoke so "negatively of federal Inspectors General charged with overseeing U.S. overseas contingency operations." She noted, "Specifically, the President expressed dismay at the IGs who '[go] over there and…do a report on every single thing that's happening, and [then] release it to the public.' He [Trump] explained that 'the public means the enemy,' who '[reads] those reports [and] studies every line of it,' and that these reports should be 'private' and 'locked up.'" Brian continued, "To further emphasize his apparent displeasure, the President called this situation 'insane' and then directed the following comment to you: 'And I don't want it to happen anymore, Mr. Secretary. You understand that.'" Brian reminded Shanahan that IGs historically played "a pivotal role in overseeing government agencies and making recommendations to prevent waste, fraud, and abuse," and that "without further clarification, [the President's] directive" to Shanahan "could lead to an unprecedented and dangerous attempt to silence these important watchdogs whose pursuit of corruption and waste saves the government billions of dollars."

In 2017, inspectors general received a half-million hotline tips. That same year, 21,500 cases were closed and there were 4,383 successful criminal prosecutions. According to the Council of Inspectors General's annual report to Congress, that same year IG offices were responsible for identifying $33 billion in potential savings and close to $22 billion in recovery for taxpayers — a $22 return for every dollar of funding for the IGs.

Even before the Trump era, government accountability experts and watchdogs were maintaining that the prolonged vacancies and temporary leadership were eroding IG effectiveness. In November 2016, Horowitz and CIGIE Vice Chair and National Science Foundation Inspector General Allison Lerner appealed in a letter to Senate leaders in both parties to do what they could to move IG confirmations through. "A sustained absence of permanent leadership for any office, particularly one entrusted with the important and challenging mission of an Office of Inspector General (OIG), is neither prudent nor reflective of good governance," the letter stated. "No matter how able or experienced an acting inspector general may be, a permanent IG has the ability to exercise more authority in setting new policies and procedures and, by virtue of the authority provided for in the IG Act, inevitably will be seen as having greater independence."

In at least two high-profile cases involving former members of Trump's Cabinet, it was a probe by an inspector general that helped set in motion the chain of events that led to their resignations. In April 2018, the EPA's IG opened an investigation into then-Administrator Scott Pruitt's use of an unprecedented around-the-clock security detail at a cost of $3 million to taxpayers. Pruitt resigned in July of that year. That October, the Department of the Interior IG referred a case the office had developed regarding then-Secretary of the Interior Ryan Zinke's role in a Montana land deal. He left two months later.

In at least one instance, though, how the government dealt with Mr. Trump's business empire came under the scrutiny of the General Services Administration's (GSA) IG. In 2013, Trump had signed a 60-year lease with the GSA for the government-owned Old Post Office Building, which Trump's real estate development company turned into the Trump International Hotel. The property is in a prime location, just blocks from the White House. In January 2019, the *Washington Business Journal* reported that the GSA's IG blasted the agency for acting "improperly" in failing to consider the constitutional issues surrounding President Donald Trump's financial stake in the entity that operates the Old Post Office hotel property. "The IG's report found the GSA ignored the issue of emoluments," an issue that flared up even before the President was sworn in, when its Office of General Counsel decided, in mid-December 2016, not to address the issue, the newspaper reported.

In May of 2018, as Trump tried to upend the IGs, he issued three executive orders to try to force the federal unions out of the workplace, where they had been since President Kennedy had signed the executive order granting federal employees the right to collectively bargain. Trump sought to dramatically reduce the presence of federal unions by targeting "release time," which permits union representatives — who are also federal employees — to represent their co-workers during regular business hours. Some federal agencies, including the Veterans Administration, the Department of Education, and the Environmental Protection Agency, implemented the executive orders. Agencies have also preempted the collective-bargaining process by having impasses declared without substantial negotiations taking place, then just imposing new contracts.

According to Everett Kelley, president of the AFGE, it would be Trump's driving unions out of federal workplaces that would inadvertently help to spread the COVID-19 virus, putting both civil servants and the public at greater risk. "This administration had taken away the ability of management and the union to work together to resolve issues," he said in a wide-ranging phone interview on May 15, 2020. "And I believe that if that had not happened, we would not have seen the extreme spread of this infection. The agencies across the board have denied us the opportunity for management and the union to partner together as we have done in the past to resolve issues."

"Up until this administration, there was a kind of collaboration, a kind of understanding" and mutual respect, no matter which political party was in the White House, Kelley observed. "But it appears this administration is hell-bent on busting unions, so that there are no checks and balances."

Throughout the pandemic, the administration rebuffed the union's efforts to slow the spread of the virus, rejecting calls for personal protective equipment and employee testing, he noted. Weeks before COVID-19 gained traction in states like New York and the nation's congregate-care facilities, it had shown up in the air-transportation sector — even as President Trump repeatedly downplayed the seriousness of the virus, comparing it to the flu.

On March 10, 2020, the Transportation Security Administration (TSA) used a tweet to announce that "three Transportation Security Officers who work at Mineta San Jose International Airport have tested positive for the COVID-19 virus." Four days earlier, officials had confirmed that two British Airways baggage handlers at London's Heathrow Airport had tested positive for coronavirus, requiring the testing of their co-workers.

On March 12, 2020, AFGE blasted the TSA for not doing enough to protect officers and the flying public from COVID-19. It called upon TSA Administrator David Pekoske to provide workers on the "front-line" with N95 protective masks. "Despite our union's numerous requests for adequate masks and protective equipment, TSA has failed to properly equip our officers with the resources they need to prevent infection," Kelley said in a statement at the time.

The agency denied the request. It was not until May 7th, after several TSA screeners had died, that the agency implemented an on-the-job mask requirement, a policy that private-sector airline carriers had begun adopting weeks earlier.

On April 3rd, the CDC rescinded its initial COVID-19 guidance against members of the public wearing masks, noting that additional research had revealed that 25 percent of those with the coronavirus showed no symptoms but could easily spread the disease. "This means that the virus can spread between people interacting in close proximity — for example, speaking, coughing, or sneezing — even if those people are not exhibiting symptoms," the agency said in a statement. "In light of this new evidence, CDC recommends wearing cloth face coverings in public settings where other social-distancing measures are difficult to maintain."

Kelley said his union's initial fight with the TSA had been over personal protective equipment, but the next round was about getting the tens of thousands of TSA workers tested for the COVID-19 virus

— something he claimed the agency still resisted, even as transportation agencies like the New York Metropolitan Transportation Authority and New Jersey Transit had embraced it. "These airport screeners might be infected and not know it, because they are not testing them," he said. "This means that as the flying public comes through every day that passes, the virus can get passed on that way." The AFGE had to fight similar battles across the nation with multiple federal agencies, he said.

Congregate-living facilities operated by the Veterans Administration and the Federal Bureau of Prisons became hotbeds for the deadly virus, which is particularly lethal for those with pre-existing health conditions. There were well over a thousand veteran and inmate COVID-19 deaths, and dozens of federal workers perished in the first few months of the virus' outbreak.

"It appears that they [Trump administration] don't want to know the truth at this point," Kelley said at the time. "It has come to the point where, in this administration, where we have agency heads telling their subordinates, 'I don't want you to tell me how many deaths there are,' which continues to put our members' and their families' lives at risk."

He contended that "denial as a strategy" was not confined to the federal government, but that Trump's direct attack on worker safety had gained traction at the state level, where governments were blocking-and-tackling for the corporations while an infectious airborne virus tore through the essential workforce and spread the disease in communities coast to coast.

In Nebraska, Kelley said, Republican Governor Pete Ricketts refused to disclose the COVID-19 employee infection rates in meat-packing plants, even though across the country such plants had proven to be incubators for the virus. "He was hiding the infection rate from the public, and that does not make the infection go away," Kelley said. "If anything, it helps this deadly virus spread, by giving the public a false sense of security." The US Department of Agriculture (USDA) disclosed that, as of May 5, 2020, 197 federal meat inspectors had been infected, with deaths reported in New York, Illinois, Mississippi, and Kansas.

To this day, there's been no full accounting for the number of frontline civil servants who died as a consequence of their service to the American people during the pandemic. There's no analysis being done about the toll on their households, although my own reporting uncovered instances where a civil servant's bout with COVID brought death home to their household.

Unions that represent the postal workers welcomed a February 9, 2021, letter from members of Congress to U.S. Postal Service (USPS) leadership on what they maintained had been the failure of management to keep their members safe during the pandemic while hiding the deadly consequences to limit the agency's liability. In the letter, Rep. Carolyn Maloney, Chair of the House Oversight and Reform Committee, pressed Postmaster General Louis DeJoy for more information about his agency's response to the "alarmingly high numbers of coronavirus infections and deaths suffered by postal workers during this pandemic." Maloney continued, "We also request that you take proactive steps to provide greater transparency and more effective mitigation of the health risks faced by the postal workforce," in the letter co-signed by Rep. Gerald E. Connolly, Chair of the Subcommittee on Government Operations.

"They are not being transparent with the rate of virus infection nor the body count," said Jonathan Smith, president of the New York Metro Area Postal Union, which represents 5,000 postal workers in New York and New Jersey. "And I am convinced the reason why the USPS does not want to reveal the truth about these COVID cases is because to do so would help our more-severely ill members to make a successful workers' compensation claim — because they won't be able to prove the nexus between their illness and their contraction of the virus on the job." He noted that the USPS's policies exposed union members unnecessarily to the virus, which has killed close to 600,000 Americans and infected well over 34 million, as of this writing.

"They say masks are mandatory; yet, if a member of the public refuses to wear a mask, our member has to serve them," Smith said.

"And you have the managers and supervisors hide in the back, while our window clerks are forced into the lobby to deal with the ire of the customers." He continued, "The postal employee understands the risk they are taking. What USPS management fails to understand is the anxiety and the stress our members feel about potentially infecting their elderly parent, their children, or other members of their household."

"By late summer 2020, ProPublica reported, more than 50,000 workers had taken time off because they were sick, had to quarantine, or had to care for a family member," the *Baltimore Sun* recounted. "The [American Postal Workers Union] says 160 postal workers have died from COVID-19, and that number might be higher by now."

An email query to the USPS's media communications office seeking confirmation of the number of COVID deaths and a reaction to the congressional inquiry into the agency's pandemic response did not get a response when I was reporting the story for *The Chief-Leader*.

The impact of what Trump had done to the federal workforce was done in full public view; but a corporatist news media, protecting the status quo, ignored the plight of working people and instead made it all about the ups-and-downs of partisan politics. And so, in 2021, after the January 6th violent insurrection in the US Capitol — just as with Trump's election in 2016 — the media oracles would say nobody saw it coming. What they missed was the very real, existential threat to the public health and to democracy that the Trump cabal posed — and even "in exile" still poses.

Chapter 8: Collective Action in Action

While former Secretary of State Hillary Clinton took the fall for Donald Trump's 2016 upset election victory, most of the nation's labor leaders who opted to back her as a "sure thing" should have realized how disconnected they were from their rank-and-file. Instead of getting behind Senator Bernie Sanders, who consistently held a commanding lead over Trump in head-to-head matchups, the unions opted to play it safe with corporatist Democrats who had been playing them for years as wages lagged and their clout increasingly diminished.

The then-74-year-old Vermont firebrand just did not have all of Clinton's baggage on free trade, Clinton Foundation self-dealing, and the six-figure speeches she gave to Goldman Sachs and others on Wall Street that had pillaged Main Street for fun and profit during the Great Recession. Yet, for most of the leadership of the nation's unions, Clinton appeared to be more electable, because they believed that Sanders' democratic socialism was too radical for the so-called American mainstream, where they assumed they needed to be strong in order to win the election.

Not since the Reagan Revolution has the leadership of organized labor been so repudiated by the vote totals in the very states and counties that data would have indicated they should be able to deliver to the Democratic candidate. NBC reported, in 2016, that Trump flipped 225 counties that President Obama had carried in 2012, in states like Michigan, Ohio, and Pennsylvania, where union registration is well above the national average. Yet, the exit polls indicated that the rank-and-file union voters split with their leadership over who should lead the country.

NBC exit polls documented that in Ohio, which had gone with Obama in 2008 and 2012, Trump's anti-free-trade stance and messaging on the economy carried the day — with union households that Romney had lost to Obama by 23 points.[101] Four years later, Trump carried those same union households by six points. For these communities, the loss of well-paid factory jobs to global free trade was life-altering, with generational consequences the "elites" had missed.

The corporate news media had to concede that the Trump working-class wave had come from states like Ohio, Pennsylvania, and Michigan, where the damage done to the Main Street economy by the Great Recession (or Great Wall Street Heist) had been far more extensive and enduring than they had reported. If the media did not see Donald Trump coming, it was because they had become entirely disconnected from the circumstances of working-class Americans.

The alleged "Recovery" that President Obama had hoped would be a cornerstone of his legacy made the banks more than whole, but it left many Midwest "rust-belt" households twisting in the wind. Whatever income gains there were went overwhelmingly to the top one percent.

Not surprisingly, the places where Donald Trump made inroads with union households were the counties that had not recovered from the financial crisis; and, in many cases, they had already been in decline since before the Great Recession. As I reported at the time, the National Association of Counties had documented that a full recovery had actually only occurred in seven percent of America's more than 3,000 counties.[102]

Significantly, there were unions that were more in touch with this growing working-class anger and had backed Senator Sanders. They knew that Clinton had everything going for her, except the arc of history. The Communication Workers of America, The American Postal Workers Union, the National Nurses United, the Amalgamated Transit Union, and Transport Workers Union (TWU)

Local 100, which represents New York City's transit workers, had all backed Sanders.

After the election, I interviewed TWU Local 100 President John Samuelsen, who went on to become the union's international president. As Samuelsen saw it, Trump's vocal opposition to the proposed Trans-Pacific Partnership free-trade pact and his pledge to roll back NAFTA wooed millions of union households looking for a shake-up of the political status quo after Obama's "hope and change" was something they could not take to the bank. "I think that it is now absolutely clear the Democratic Party has lost touch with its working-class roots," Samuelsen told me at the time. "These fissures in the working class have been exploited and blown wide open by Donald Trump. Democrats need to take a step back and ask why, with all the ridiculous things Trump said, was he ultimately more palatable to working-class trade-union Democrats?"

The post-2016 challenge for organized labor was to re-energize itself and insert a new militancy into the national conversation — which was exactly what 20,000 West Virginia teachers stepped up and did, starting in February 2018, with a strike across that state's 55 counties that shuttered its schools. The two-week strike in the staunchly Republican and right-to-work state mobilized by teachers from the American Federation of Teachers (AFT) and the National Education Association (NEA) was successfully brought to an end when the state's Republican Governor James C. Justice signed off on giving the teachers a five-percent raise.

According to *The New York Times*, the West Virginia teachers were "among the lowest paid in the nation," had not had a raise for four years, and were pressed to the margins — like so many other Americans, grappling with the unrelenting rise in healthcare costs. "Teachers across the state came together for one goal," Renita Benson, a reading teacher from Calhoun County, told *The New York Times*, as teachers gathered to celebrate their victory in the state capital. "It's not the raise as much as it is having the respect that we deserve from the government, and I think that was proven today."

A key ingredient was the way the teachers' unions organized local, daily food provisioning programs throughout the strike, with a caring consciousness for the students and families that would have been directly deprived of the school-provided lunch — and often breakfast — on which so many of them relied for sustenance. West Virginia was an inflection point. Those teachers inspired their fellow teachers to strike in Oklahoma, Arizona, Colorado, North Carolina, and Kentucky.

Despite the rising tide of labor militancy, though, by that winter holiday season, Trump thought nothing of cutting the paychecks for hundreds of thousands of federal workers — many of whom had voted for him —and requiring a significant number of them to continue to work without pay. If ever there was a time for labor leadership to illustrate just how phony the Trump and GOP's alliance was with working-class Americans, this was it.

Yet, in the face of this moral injury Trump had done to loyal federal employees, America's labor movement was relatively passive. There were some shows of solidarity for the American Federation of Government Employees (AFGE) and the National Treasury Employees Union (NTEU), but no one was publicly suggesting shutting down the country to drive home Trump's recklessness and cruelty. The Bully-in-Chief was on a roll.

It wasn't until January 20, 2019, when a national labor leader — Association of Flight Attendants (AFA) CWA International President Sara Nelson[103] — gave an impassioned speech suggesting a general strike.[104] "Almost a million workers are locked out or being forced to work without pay. Others are going to work when our workspace is increasingly unsafe," she said. "What is the Labor Movement waiting for?"

Nelson invoked the memory of Dr. Martin Luther King, Jr., who had been willing to take risks on behalf of the labor movement, as he did by going to Memphis on behalf of striking sanitation workers in 1968. The occasion of her speech was her acceptance of the 2019 AFL-CIO MLK Drum Major for Justice Award in Washington, DC. "We need to follow Dr. King's lead and think big," Nelson said. "Think big, like the hotel workers who took on the largest hotel chain in the world and won. Think big, like the teachers in Los Angeles who, this very minute, are taking on powerful hedge funds to save public education for our children."

She continued, "Federal-sector unions have their hands full, caring for the 800,000 federal workers who are at the tip of the spear. Some would say the answer is for them to walk off the job. I say, 'what are you willing to do?' Their destiny IS tied up with our destiny — and they don't even have time to ask us for help. Don't wait for an invitation. Get engaged, join or plan a rally, get on a picket line, organize sit-ins at lawmakers' offices.... Go back with the Fierce Urgency of NOW to talk with your Locals and International unions about all workers joining together — to end this shutdown with a general strike."

Since the 1981 mass firing by President Reagan of the striking air traffic controllers, union participation has been on the decline — with the exception of a half-point increase in union density in 2020, up to 10.8 percent. By contrast, in the early 1980s, one in five American workers were represented by a union.[105] It should come as no shock that there's a direct historical connection between the decline in union enrollment, depressed wages, and rising inequality.[106] Regardless of which party was in charge, these circumstances have continued to worsen. In the private sector, by 2020, just 6.3 percent of workers were represented by a union. In the public sector, 34.8 percent of workers are represented.

In my interview with her in May 2021, Nelson recalled that, before her general strike speech, she had been consumed from the start of the shutdown with how to end it. "Back when it first started on December 21st, 2018, I was focused on trying to end it, because I knew what it would do to our industry and how it was going to affect the people that I represent and the people who care for them — the air traffic controllers, the TSA agents — and so I was working on getting the industry united," Nelson said.

Nelson helped bring together an industry-wide coalition that included labor unions, the airlines, plane manufacturers, the airports — basically the entirety of the aviation industry —who all signed on to a January 2019 letter to the White House and Congress, laying out what the broader economic consequences would be of the ongoing federal government shutdown. "It was historic and unprecedented," Nelson recalled; and yet, the government remained shuttered. "I was thinking, what else do I need to do? Would anyone give a shit if I went on a hunger strike and chained myself to the Capitol?!"

The New York Times reported that, four days later, remarks that Ms. Nelson made at Reagan National Airport — in support of the federal workers who were going without pay in high-stress positions, like air traffic controllers — went viral. "Many of these people are our veterans," Ms. Nelson told the crowd. "Many of these people are fighting for our country right now, and we are not paying them."

The *Times* reported, "The next day, a handful of air traffic controllers on the East Coast did not show up to work, briefly grounding flights in New York. Hours later, President Trump announced a deal to reopen the government."

"Between you and me, that's what ended the shutdown, you know," Senator Bernie Sanders told Nelson in his office, according to the *Times.*

Nelson herself noted how ironic it was that air traffic controllers would deal Trump one of his more high-profile embarrassments, when 35 days into his shutdown, on January 25th, he had to fold after some of them called in sick and started an aviation nightmare scenario that started in New York's airspace and was spreading by the hour. "Air traffic controllers go into a dark room, and nobody ever sees them, and nobody ever thinks about them," Nelson said. "People are happy not to think about them." She continued, "The thing I think that was most important was putting that threat out there directly; then they [the Trump White House] started to see it happen, and they could not let labor taste our power. And so, that was it."

In an interview several months into the pandemic, Nelson said she believed the national public crisis provided "essential workers" with an unprecedented opportunity to improve their circumstances and regain that leverage they had lost since the Reagan era. "So, [the term] 'essential workers' is basically like a 'please don't strike now' plea from the corporate elite; because we really have all the power," she said.

Nelson grew up in a household where her family regularly attended the Church of Christ, Scientist— founded by a woman, Mary Baker Eddy — where God was spoken of in non-patriarchal mother/father terms. "So, it wasn't until I got into the workplace — and even more so in the labor movement — that I had any real consciousness of the disparities between men and women," she said. "But my foundation was that I had complete equal standing with anyone else in the room. And I think that serves me well, even though it has been really hurtful learning the reality of the situation."

For Nelson, it was being in a union "that made all the difference in the world — it was the union that made this job into a career. The union was formed to beat back all of these discriminatory practices."

The AFA, formed in 1945, got its first contract in 1946, which provided a seniority list that, Nelson says, was the basis "for every other win on equality and equity, because managers could no longer expect sexual favors to trade for schedules. It was based on a system that was transparent." She continued, "When I started, there absolutely was a sense we were going to stand on our own feet — which we had the ability to do, because of our union. But no one else respected us; and we had to know that we were going to have to fight it out every single time."

The #MeToo movement had special resonance for Nelson and her fellow flight attendants, because the issue was something that "was so isolating for women — you just didn't talk about those things. They are embarrassing. They were meant to be embarrassing. They were intended to be a way to make you be quiet; and all of a sudden, we could talk about this as a shared experience.

"A fraction of flight attendants had ever, up to that point, reported sexual harassment issues; and I started talking to other flight attendants about this and about how pervasive it was," she said. "Flight attendants had this view that this was just part of the job, and we just deal with it. Now, we deal with it in different ways — taking care of each other, standing our ground, and pushing people back — and demanding we get certification from the FAA and that we be recognized by our government as critical to the aviation industry."

She was elected president of the AFA in 2014. Five years later, that speech she gave, accepting the AFL-CIO MLK Drum Major for Justice Award in Washington, D.C., sparked serious talk of her becoming a candidate in the June 2022 contest for AFL-CIO president — a run she is still pondering, as of this writing.

More than a year into the pandemic, researchers with the Institute for Policy Studies documented that half of the nation's 100 largest low-wage employers had rigged their own CEO compensation rules to give their CEOs, on average, a 29 percent raise, while giving their frontline workers a two-percent decrease. IPS reported that in this cohort of CEOs, compensation averaged $15.3 million while the median pay for their workforce was $28,187— two percent lower than in 2019.

"If you look at that list, the only executives you won't see are the airlines' CEOs," Nelson said. With some pride, she added that her union, along with the other airline industry unions, had insisted on prohibitions for such excesses in the Payroll Protection Program that Congress had passed to keep the airline industry intact during the pandemic. "I'd been through this before, after 9/11, with the corporate elite always willing to use a crisis to try and get workers to work harder for less and to put more money in their pocket," she said. "We were not going to let a crisis ratchet down the value of our work; and, at the same time, there was a cap on executive compensation that stays in place two years after the relief ends. And it also bans stock buybacks."

As the airline unions demonstrated with the Payroll Protection Program, it's possible — when labor is united — to check the excesses of corporate capitalism to the benefit of workers.

"Every single one of us came together and put a massive concentrated political effort into Washington, D.C., so there was an incredible amount of solidarity in defense of our collective membership," said John Samuelsen, president of the Transport Workers Union International, which represents 150,000 workers in the airline, railroad, and mass-transit sectors. "We had the IAM [International Association of Machinists], the CWA, the TWU and the ATU, the Transportation Trades Department of the AFL-CIO, all united with one singular purpose in this drive. And that was to ensure that any money going from the federal government went to the workforce, not to the purchase of stock options or executive pay raises."

In contrast, the overwhelming majority of working Americans have no union. Indeed, a growing percentage are considered so-called "gig workers," without even the basic labor protections that date back to the 1930s — when overtime, disability, unemployment, and all Social Security benefits became part of the social contract for anyone that was employed.

Add in the millions of undocumented immigrant workers, operating in the margins of society and so vulnerable to exploitation, and it easy to see just how much leverage capital interests have in an economy defined by scarcity, where workers are so often set up to undercut each other merely to survive.

We have been here before, when the forces of capital continued to press their advantage by continuing to squeeze the working families who generated their wealth, and the government — captive to those same interests — stood idly by or, as in the case of several strikes, used military force against the workers.

That was the case when Woodrow Wilson sent federal troops to Colorado at the request of the governor, who had used his National Guard to violently suppress a strike by thousands of miners against the Colorado Fuel & Iron Corporation, owned by the Rockefeller family. As historian Howard Zinn recounts, that state-sanctioned violence, known as the Ludlow Massacre, resulted in the killing of 11 children and two women. Historical accounts of what ensued are now referenced as the 1913-1914 Colorado Coalfield War, which targeted the United Mine Workers and left scores of workers dead.

Just over a century ago, Wilson — singularly focused on winning World War I — also suppressed information about a catastrophically deadly pandemic and left to local authorities the public health response to the so-called "Spanish Flu." In the early 20th century, it was Wilson who would play the role of Donald Trump. Wilson was a Democrat who had been elected governor of New Jersey; and he was also a white supremacist. Throughout that 1918-1920 pandemic, it was President Woodrow Wilson who concealed the killer disease from the American people, even as it devoured them, killing 675,000 here and tens of millions worldwide. Then, as now — as measured by average life expectancy — the health of the American people had been declining for three years ahead of that mass-death event.[107] In Wilson's case, the rationale for suppressing any awareness of the disease was to avoid undermining the war effort. We refer to that pandemic as the "Spanish Flu" only because it was that country's press — which was not subject to, or coordinated with, Wilson's wartime press restrictions — that reported on it. Tragically, and as a practical matter, more American soldiers would end up dying from the Spanish Flu than in combat. Yet, to this day, our historic recollection continues to obscure Wilson's deceit.

But the historic corollary does not end there. Even as Wilson, who had run on a pledge to keep the United States out of war, was building consensus for it, a small army of suffragettes led by Alice Paul and others, was taking residence in Lafayette Park, outside the White House, to press for the vote for women.[108] Alice Paul, who was born to Quaker parents in Mount Laurel, New Jersey, was the leading architect of the 1913 Women's Procession that brought thousands of women to Washington, D.C., in what was an unprecedented protest for those times.[109] As a master of the media and the use of images to convey a political message, Paul led a persistent presence outside the White House in 1917, which the protestors maintained for 18 months. The disciplined cadre of women became known as the "silent sentinels," because they refused to be deterred by the near constant heckling to which they were subjected. It was that era's Occupy movement.

According to the Alice Paul Institute's webpage, "In January 1917, Paul and over 1,000 'Silent Sentinels' began eighteen months of picketing the White House, standing at the gates with such signs as, 'Mr. President, how long must women wait for liberty?'.... They endured verbal and physical attacks from spectators, which increased after the US entered World War I."[110]

The institute's narrative continues, "Instead of protecting the women's right to free speech and peaceful assembly, the police

114

arrested them on the flimsy charge of obstructing traffic. Paul was sentenced to jail for seven months, where she organized a hunger strike in protest. "Doctors threatened to send Paul to an insane asylum and force-fed her, while newspaper accounts of her treatment garnered public sympathy and support for suffrage. By 1918, Wilson announced his support for suffrage."

As you will read in the chapters ahead, though, there are signs of an ascendant, broad-based, multiracial movement that has grown more powerful in the crucible of a pandemic and in the face of the rising threat of racist authoritarianism. Women are central to this movement, as exemplified by Representative Alexandria Ocasio-Cortez's 2018 win over a longtime Democratic incumbent. She is one of the scores of women who are getting involved and winning, and they are redefining our politics in the process. This movement is not just playing out in the electoral sphere, but even within the union movement itself, as a new generation takes the controls. In many ways, we have been here before — when the confluence of traumatic events has either broken or emboldened us — advancing the human condition and inching us closer to a more inclusive version of "We the People."

Chapter 9: Harnessing the Power of the Powerless

So, how do we break out of the Stuck Nation cycle and empower the tens of millions of Americans marginalized by economic exploitation in a racist and misogynistic system that puts the accumulation of wealth above all other human endeavors? America's one-percent wealth-building and -preservation machine uses advertising to harness and corral our imagination as to what success looks like. Luxury is success, and poverty is failure. For generations now, we have been counseling our children on what to study in college based on what will bring them the most money. For tens of millions of Americans, this has meant taking on crippling debt on a bet that their "investment" will turn a profit sometime during their working life.

"We must rapidly begin the shift from a "thing" oriented society to a "person" oriented society," wrote Dr. Martin Luther King, Jr., in his 1967 book *Where Do We Go from Here*. "When machines and computers, profit motives and property rights are considered more important than people, the giant triplets of racism, materialism and militarism are incapable of being conquered. A civilization can flounder as readily in the face of moral and spiritual bankruptcy as it can through financial bankruptcy." In the next paragraph, King asks that we "honestly admit that capitalism has often left a gulf between superfluous wealth and abject poverty," which "created conditions permitting necessities to be taken from the many to give luxuries to the few." More than a half-century ago, King was anticipating the "dislocations" that automation and technology would mean for workers. "The displaced are flowing into proliferating service occupations," he wrote in 1967. "These enterprises are traditionally

117

unorganized and provide low wage scales with longer hours." King saw the union movement as the way for the mass of all working people — regardless of race or religion — to assert themselves in such a way, collectively, that they could no longer be ignored. By prevailing in this struggle to be visible, workers become a force to be reckoned with by the "owners" and gain the agency to shape their own destiny — a power that cannot be achieved in isolation. By becoming the subject of the narrative, we take back our power to shape our history going forward.

It's no accident that the history of the American labor movement is missing from what is generally taught in our schools, when it comes to our national history that's been so long framed by the "great white men." Even in reflecting on the history of King and the Civil Rights Movement, all too often the story of the workers who were central to that struggle can be lost in the shadows of the retrospective spotlight.

So, it is with the sanitation workers in Memphis, Tennessee — Echol Cole, 36, and Robert Walker, 30 — who were both crushed to death on February 1, 1968, inside an antiquated and unsafe garbage collection truck, about which workers had long complained. According to King biographer Taylor Branch, Cole and Walker had sought refuge in the truck during a torrential downpour, because the city's racist zoning laws prohibited "shelter stops in residential neighborhoods, after citizen complaints about unsightly 'picnics' by the Negro sanitation workers."

"For years, Black sanitation workers had complained about unsafe working conditions and poverty wages," recounts Wendi C. Thomas for the MLK50, Justice through Journalism project. "At least three times — in 1963, 1964 and 1966 — they faced retaliation from bosses while trying to unionize or planning to go on strike."

The brutal and unnecessary deaths of Cole and Walker, in the prime of their young lives, prompted 1,300 of their co-workers to strike on Lincoln's Birthday, February 12, 1968. Their strike went on to spark the "I am a Man" mobilization, which brought King to Memphis, in

118

support of the American Federation of State, County and Municipal Employees recognition campaign. Ultimately, in the weeks after King's assassination in Memphis that April 4th, the city would agree to settle the strike, raise the workers' pay, and recognize their union.

Previously, in November 1967, King had used the occasion of a staff retreat for the Southern Christian Leadership Conference to announce the launch of his "Poor People's Campaign," which was aimed at bringing together a multiracial coalition building on existing organizing efforts rooted in poor Native American, Latino, Black, and rural communities. That movement had much in common with the dynamics of the labor union movement, which achieved success by getting individual workers to identify with their co-workers and to see the advance of their collective agenda as in their personal self-interest.

It was the fear that King and his supporters could achieve such a synergy that earned the Civil-Rights leader the enmity of FBI Director Jay Edgar Hoover. King's controversial linking of the Civil-Rights struggle to a broader critique, which included his opposition to the Vietnam War and to the nation's stratified economic system, was considered a threat to national security and the existing social order. The roots of Hoover's mandate harken back to the Cold War anti-communist purges that played out in every facet of American life, from the backlots of Hollywood to labor-union hiring halls, and even reached into academic ivory towers.

The Bureau described King as the "most dangerous and effective Negro leader in the country," with Hoover telling the Kennedy White House that key King advisors were actually communist agents. In 1963, then-US Attorney General Robert Kennedy, who had also briefly worked for Wisconsin Senator Joseph McCarthy, the anti-communist demagogue, signed off on the FBI's covert surveillance of King. Those operations, along with Hoover's COINTELPRO program — which targeted a long list of activists and groups like the Black Panthers — was a secret effort to derail a political convergence that the FBI feared would upend America's existing power structure and its economic system.

A half-century after King's assassination, the economic stratification he preached against has become even more pronounced. Even leaders in the capitalist establishment, like Federal Reserve Chairman Jerome Powell and Treasury Secretary Janet Yellen, have stated that our current levels of wealth and income inequality are a growing risk to the viability of the economy.

Historically, even as the percentage of unionized workers declined after President Reagan fired the air traffic controllers, union membership has meant significantly higher wages, according to the Bureau of Labor Statistics. For years now, unions like the Service Employees International Union (SEIU) have been focusing on the service sector and immigrant workers, regardless of their legal status, with their campaign for a $15 minimum wage.

Today, King's work of building a multiracial coalition to address poverty is being carried forward by the Poor People's Campaign: A National Call for a Moral Revival, which is co-chaired by Reverend Dr. William Barber and now has more than 40 state-based committees working to advance the interests of this growing constituency.

In an interview several months into the COVID pandemic, Barber reflected on the increasingly stratified nature of America: "62 million people make less than a living wage in this country — 140 million people were poor and low wealth before COVID ever got started," said Barber. "We know that these were the people that were the face-to-face workers who were the first to have to go back to work, the first to get sick, and the first to die. They can't be the last to be lifted up."

Barber says building a vibrant labor movement is an essential part of a multifaceted strategy aimed at countering the efforts by state legislatures to both suppress voter turnout and limit access to the voting franchise. "Unionizing these workers; giving them collective bargaining power in these anti-labor, so-called 'right-to-work' states; addressing voter suppression; and fighting for a living wage are key to building the coalition that can have the political power for the rising of a new South, a new Midwest, a new Rust Belt," Barber said. "Here's my point: Poor and low-wealth [people] — fusing coalitions between Black, white, brown, and Indigenous people — are the key to transforming the South. And the South is key to transforming the nation.... You can't build that coalition without dealing with systemic racism and poverty together."

He continued, "You can't just talk about racism in terms of police reform. You've got to talk about it in terms of education, re-segregation, disparity in wages, and healthcare; and then you have to show poor and low-wealth whites that the very people that pass racist voter-suppression laws — once they get elected — use that power to block living wages."

In March 2021, Barber spoke directly to the intersectionality of these issues in a rally leading up to the Amazon unionization vote in Bessemer, Alabama, which the company ultimately defeated — but the results are being challenged by the Retail, Wholesale and Department Store Union. During our interview, Barber expressed disappointment when, in March 2021, several Senate Democrats joined all of the Senate's Republicans to reject Senator Bernie Sanders' amendment to make a $15 minimum wage part of President Biden's American Rescue Plan. Barber urged Biden, whom he said he "respected and loved," to be more like "Franklin Delano Roosevelt, who used his bully pulpit and said in the middle of the Great Depression that any business that did not want to pay a living wage did not deserve to be a business in America. Well, poor and low-wealth people have been in a Depression…. We know that right now, as you and I are speaking, there are 62 million poor and low-wealth workers in this country."

Barber likened the Senate to a "House of Lords," disconnected from the daily experiences of the tens of millions of poor and low-wealth Americans. "It took Black people 400 years to get to $7.25 — we can't wait another 400 years," he said, to get to a $15 minimum wage. "What they are doing should embolden us and intensify the agitation. If we challenged Trump for using power in the wrong way, then we have to challenge our own 'friends,' the people we voted for. We did not vote for 'normalcy.' We did not vote for the same." If Democrats fail to deliver on the $15 minimum wage as they promised, Barber warns, they could suffer the same fate in next year's midterm elections that Democrats did in 2016, when a marked decline in African American voter turnout sank Hillary Clinton's campaign and handed Trump the Oval Office.[111]

For Rev. Barber, a return to a pre-COVID "normal" that so many crave is a "sign of a kind of spiraling, spiritual death" and a willful blindness to the 250,000 poor and low-wealth people that were dying every year — before the pandemic — due to inadequate or nonexistent healthcare. "We had seven people die from vaping, and we had the White House and Congress convening hearings," he said. "While with 750 people dying from poverty and low wealth every day [pre-COVID], you still couldn't get a politician to talk about poverty consistently."

So far, our nation is four-for-four in failing to address the living economic legacy of slavery. There is a through-line from Jim Crow right on through the poverty wages paid to this very day for essential services in the face-to-face workplaces where millions of people of color work. This 21st-century "Grapes of Wrath" class of worker, of course, includes millions of poor white people as well; particularly in the South and rural Midwest, along with immigrants of all races in all 50 states.

There was the reversal of Reconstruction after the Civil War, when the North let the South rise again through draconian segregation, lynching, and total voter suppression. Then, FDR allowed Southern Democrats to maintain their economically oppressive apartheid by exempting agricultural workers and domestic workers from the landmark 1938 Fair Labor Standards Act and the minimum wage, which lifted so many out of poverty but left so many behind.[112] In more recent times, there was the Bush-then-Obama response to Wall Street's hijacking of the American economy, which bailed out vulture capitalists at the expense of millions of homeowners who lost their homes, leading to a loss of household wealth that was especially consequential for generations of African Americans.[113]

And, finally, in response to the COVID pandemic, we had the $1.9 trillion American Rescue Plan Act of 2021, which allocated vast amounts of borrowed money — to be paid off by taxpayers — that ensured corporations could continue amassing huge profits while denying tens of millions a living wage. "Low wages hurt all workers and are particularly harmful to Black workers and other workers of color, especially women of color who make up a disproportionate

122

share of workers who are severely underpaid," according to an Economic Policy Institute fact sheet on the minimum wage.[114] "This is the result of structural racism and sexism, with an economic system rooted in chattel slavery in which workers of color — and especially women of color — have been and continue to be shunted into the most underpaid jobs."

When that bipartisan coalition in the US Senate rejected the $15 minimum wage in March 2021, they voted to keep it that way. As Barber sees it, that abandonment of the $15 minimum wage by centrist Democrats doesn't just reinforce systemic economic racism, it's political science malpractice.

According to Barber, 55 percent of poor and low-wealth voters cast their ballot for the Biden/Harris ticket. "We found that poor and low-wealth people make up a third of the electorate. That's 65 million voters, and 35 million voted this time — six million more than in 2016.... So that's the only place you can expand the electorate." While neoliberals within the Democratic Party may be slow to grasp the power that resides in poor and low-wealth workers, the Trump acolytes that now control Republican state legislatures are keenly aware of the risk this voting block poses to the corrupt racist political order. Consider that in state after state where this segment of voters holds the balance of power, states have enacted draconian voter-suppression measures meant to ensure there not be a replay of the 2020 US Senate run-off elections in Georgia that saw Democrats Jon Ossoff and Reverend Raphael Warnock prevail.

The head-spinning velocity with which states like Florida have moved to turn the clock back by limiting the franchise is a clear indication of just how desperate the authoritarian racists are to cling to power. The 2020 general election, which saw the repudiation at the polls of the anti-union and anti-immigrant Trump movement, also saw a record turnout enabled by the prevalence of the universal mail-in ballot.

Yet, even with the upsurge in voter participation that provided Biden a mass win at the top of the ticket, Trump's Republican Party reduced Speaker Pelosi's majority in the House and continued to dominate at the state level, where they control 61 chambers compared to 37 for the Democrats.

We can only get America unstuck by engaging the 30 million "poor and low-wealth voters" that Dr. Barber references — not just in the high-profile presidential contests every four years, but locally where access to the ballot and the right to vote itself are throttled by vested interests that profit from minority rule.

Chapter 10: We're All in the Same Boat

If the United States has been "stuck," so has its beleaguered labor movement, which — despite the best efforts of the dominant capital interests — has continued to endure into the 21st century over some pretty steep odds. Owners and speculators (those who make money with money) have resorted to all sorts of tactics — some violent, others more subtle, but equally repressive — to keep labor divided.

As a consequence, the overwhelming majority of working Americans have no union. Indeed, a growing percentage are considered "gig workers," without even the basic labor protections that date back to the1930s — when overtime, disability, unemployment, and Social Security benefits became part of the social contract for anyone that was employed. Add in the millions of undocumented immigrant workers, operating in the margins of society and so vulnerable to exploitation, and it is easy to see just how much leverage capital interests have in an economy defined by scarcity, where workers are so often set up to undercut each other merely to survive.

The more labor is divided or disorganized, the easier it is for the exploiters to rack up their profits at the expense of workers and the planet. Among other forms of fragmentation, they use false narratives to undermine worker solidarity; and, if left unchallenged, those narratives gain traction and become foundational for a right-wing, anti-immigrant worldview. One example is the widely held belief that undocumented immigrants don't pay taxes and are taking away jobs from — or freeloading on — "hardworking Americans."

In 2017, the Institute of Taxation and Economic Policy (ITEP) reported that undocumented immigrants were more than 50 percent compliant in filing income taxes, and one in three actually owned a home here and contributed almost $12 billion in state and local taxes.[115] "Undocumented immigrants nationwide pay on average an estimated 8 percent of their incomes in state and local taxes (this is their effective state and local tax rate)," ITEP researchers found. "To put this in perspective, the top 1 percent of taxpayers pay an average nationwide effective tax rate of just 5.4 percent."

Exploiting racial tensions and nativist fervor has historically been a successful management tactic, according to Joseph Wilson, a former political science professor at the City University of New York and a leading expert on the African American Civil Rights Movement. "In terms of the tensions between immigrants and African Americans, certainly management and the employer class always sought to pit ethnic groups against one another in establishing a certain color hierarchy and class pecking order," Wilson said. "The bottom strata of employment — that had previously been used as almost exclusive territory for former African American slaves — would be where immigrants would work, really as *de facto* slaves, for even less wages and risking more dangerous conditions, and that would displace Black workers."

Wilson said that for unions to be successful, they have to build multiracial and multiethnic coalitions in the tradition of A. Philip Randolph, who founded the Brotherhood of Sleeping Car Porters in the 1920s.[116] "While it was a Chinese immigrant workforce that built the Transcontinental Railroad, it was the African American porters who were pretty much slave labor in terms of railway service, because they didn't get paid wages until the establishment of their national union," Wilson said. "They lived on tips, and the only way that porters, the red caps, those who handled the baggage, and the chefs got paid was by smiling through all their pain. That's how those jobs came to be known as 'miles of smiles,' because the radiance of your smile determined your salary."

Randolph left Crescent City, Florida, for New York City in 1911, where he worked during the day and attended the City College of New York at night. In 1925, he became the general organizer of the Brotherhood of Sleeping Car Porters; but it would not be until 1937 that the mostly African American union signed a labor contract with the railroad. In 1941, Randolph was a chief organizer in the March on Washington Movement, which had the effect of forcing President Franklin Delano Roosevelt to integrate the nation's booming defense industry.

Wilson said that not all unions embraced the Civil Rights Movement. "Historically, it's been a mixed bag," he said. "The skilled trades tended to fight it, and the industrial workers tended to support it." To this day, racism and xenophobia are fissures within the union movement, as reflected in the segments of residual support for Donald Trump — even after his attempt to foment mob violence to subvert the peaceful transition of power. We can't ignore the significant presence of active public-union members and retired civil servants inside the Capitol on January 6, 2021. It's a perversely historical irony that the labor movement had listened to the likes of FBI Director J. Edgar Hoover for decades and purged socialists and communists (who were often the best organizers) because they were labeled as "a threat to national security."

Earlier in this book, I touched on how the brutality of the Triangle Shirtwaist Fire, which resulted in the horrific death of dozens of young female immigrant garment workers, galvanized a mobilization that lives on in support of worker safety, transcending any nativist fixation on a worker's origins or immigration status. In January 2017, a massive rally of 20,000 New York City union building trades members converged in Lower Manhattan, engulfing City Hall (not far from the site of the Triangle Shirtwaist Fire). The multiracial crowd reflected the progress made in that sector, since the days when Black and Latino community activists faced off with white building trade union members, in years past often coming to blows over opening up access to those high-paying trades that were too often controlled by organized crime.

The 2017 rally was convened by a private- and public-union coalition that included the leaders of New York City's Building Trades, the Uniformed Firefighters Association (UFA), the Uniformed Fire Officers Association (UFOA) and the Transport Workers Union Local 100, who all supported a City Council bill that would mandate apprentice training for all construction workers — regardless of their immigration status. The "all hands-on-deck" protest was timed to counter the well-funded efforts by the city's developers and real estate

127

interests to derail the legislation, which was drafted to address a disturbing spike in gruesome workplace deaths and injuries during the city's construction boom, often involving undocumented workers who had no healthcare or disability insurance. According to the New York Committee for Occupational Safety and Health (NYCOSH), a non-profit advocacy group, in the previous two years there had been 30 construction worksite deaths. According to NYCOSH, 90 percent of those fatalities were at non-union worksites that often rely on undocumented workers.

Jake Lemonda, president of the UFOA — a predominately white, male union — told the crowd that his members had witnessed firsthand the consequences of inadequate construction-worker training, when retrieving dead bodies from the accident scenes. "Thirty times, we had to go to a site and take that person back to their loved ones," he said. "We know, as fire officers, about training. We know the dangers we face, and we train every single day. That is what you deserve. You deserve to work in a safe environment."

"All too often, our members respond to a construction accident, and we pull up on the scene and you can tell this could have been prevented had the proper training been given to those construction workers," said UFA President Jim Slevin. "These tragedies should not be happening. Nobody should put a dollar value on the safety of construction workers." Both Lemonda's and Slevin's remarks were greeted by roars of approval from the crowd that spanned several blocks.

"We gather at City Hall today to demonstrate our support for this critically important package of bills that will protect the lives of construction workers across the five boroughs," said Gary LaBarbera, president of the Building and Construction Trades Council of Greater New York. "We can no longer tolerate irresponsible developers and contractors who are putting profits over the safety of workers. This must end now."

For years, firefighters had been responding to the carnage at non-union construction sites, where workers who lacked basic skills used counterfeit OSHA cards to suggest they were trained. The union members — no doubt, many Trump voters among them — were not chanting for the undocumented to be deported, but for them to be trained. As one man put it, "No man should die because he just wanted to feed his family."

Back in 2015, *The New York Times* had done an in-depth examination into the circumstances involved with construction-site deaths for the prior two years and confirmed "an increase in fatalities and injuries" that "mostly affected undocumented laborers" that "far exceeds the rate of new construction" over the same period. They also found that many of the deaths "were completely avoidable."

In 2016, in a sign of changing times since the acquittal a century earlier of the owners of the Triangle Shirtwaist Factory, a construction company and company official were convicted in a New York State court on criminal charges related to the April 2015 cave-in that caused the death of Carlos Moncayo — an undocumented construction worker who was buried when a 13-foot trench collapsed on him and three of his co-workers. The precarious nature of the excavation had been previously flagged by a city inspector whose warnings were ignored.

"Construction has always been and remains the most dangerous major industry in the country, and every time there is a building boom in New York City, the fatalities go up," said Mike Maguire, the political director of the Mason Tenders Council of New York. "It is very clear that the non-union workers are being treated just as disposable human beings by the contractors and developers." Maguire maintained that, in addition to superior craft training, union workers had the prerogative to challenge management over unsafe conditions. "A union worker has the freedom to say to the boss, 'I am not going up on that unsafe scaffold; I am not going down into that unshorn-up trench,'" he said. "What we have here is largely an undocumented workforce that is threatened every day with being deported or with losing their job." Those fears can far outweigh an undocumented worker's interest in raising concerns about safety, asking for training, or seeking other rights or benefits provided to represented workers.

Joshua B. Freeman, labor historian and Professor Emeritus of History at the City University of New York Graduate Center, saw labor's support of the bill as part of a trend that "started to really happen some time ago — when the center of gravity within the labor movement had shifted and the AFL-CIO, and many of its constituent unions, moved away from trying to limit undocumented immigration to...embrace all workers, whether or not they were documented, both because they were workers and to keep them from undercutting conditions for other workers."

The January 2017 coalition of uniformed first responders, the building trades, and the transit workers that came together to lift up undocumented construction workers was also a direct outgrowth of their previous experience in working together to win passage of the legislation that created the World Trade Center Health Program and the 9/11 Victims Compensation Fund.

"In today's polarized social environment, it's absolutely essential for organized labor's survival and growth to dynamically engage with undocumented immigrant communities," said Professor and labor historian Joseph Wilson. "In fact, so-called 'undocumented communities' are synonymous with, and largely indistinguishable from, broader working-class communities of color, especially in the urban service sectors and extending to rural agricultural communities."

As referenced earlier, some of New York State's biggest unions played a leading role in the 2021 passage of a $2.1 billion relief bill for hundreds of thousands of undocumented workers who lost their jobs during the COVID-19 pandemic and were excluded from the American Rescue Plan. The program, agreed to as part of the state budget deal, is the first of its kind. Dubbed the Excluded Worker Fund Act, it will provide thousands of dollars in wage-replacement aid for immigrant workers who can't collect unemployment. Unions, including Service Employees International Union (SEIU) Locals 1199 and 32BJ, District Council 37 and Communications Workers of America District 1, joined 150 immigrant-rights groups and community-based organizations in a letter to Governor Cuomo and state legislative leaders urging them to adopt the measure.

The letter stated, "Many excluded workers worked in essential jobs serving and protecting the rest of us during the peaks of the pandemic; yet if they became too ill to continue working, or lost their jobs or hours as businesses shuttered, they still were blocked from accessing the basic unemployment relief that the rest of us depend on to survive during the darkest times." The letter noted that "undocumented immigrants' employers have contributed over $1.4 billion into the unemployment system over the past 10 years on behalf of workers that are not eligible to collect." Other union signatories included the New York State Nurses Association; the Retail, Wholesale and Department Store Union; the Professional Staff Congress; the New York Taxi Workers Alliance; and the Construction & General Building Laborers' Local 79. Maritza Silva-Farrell, the executive director of ALIGN, a labor- and immigrant-rights group, said in a statement, "From the beginning of the COVID-19 pandemic, New York's more than two million essential workers have been on the front lines helping to keep the rest of us safe, and more than half of them are undocumented immigrants....Now, these same workers have made history, winning the first-in-the-nation excluded workers fund for New York State."

Even before the pandemic, the undocumented and immigrant workforce had become foundational to the country's healthcare-delivery system. A recent Harvard Medical School study found that three million immigrants account for roughly 25 percent of the nation's healthcare workforce, according to *U.S. News and World Report*. The analysis included staffing, not only in hospitals, but in long-term-care facilities and in the rapidly growing home-healthcare sector where workers are often hired directly by families. "About 27% of direct care workers — home health and personal care nurses and aides — are immigrants, and immigrants also account for a full 30% of the housekeeping and maintenance workers at nursing homes," the publication reported.

About 13 percent of the nursing-home workforce performing housekeeping, construction, and maintenance consists of undocumented immigrants. Keith Joseph is a vice-president of SEIU 1199 and represents 80,000 home-healthcare workers throughout New York State. Many of his members are from immigrant families in which there can be US citizens, green-card holders and undocumented individuals all living under the same roof. After a 2019 rally to protest the Trump administration anti-immigrant policies, Joseph told me that, because of the industry's low wages, it was not uncommon for caregivers to have to turn to some form of public assistance to fill the gap — which under Trump's proposals could result in them being denied green card status.

"They do not come here for a handout," he said. "They come here to work and work hard; and the jobs they do, the average person who is a US citizen born here would not do. They do not complain; and they uplift themselves and their families, while they build community all at the same time." He continued, "They work based on the hours they get, and sometimes they don't get the hours that are needed. They don't have a choice but to try and get some assistance…and we must protect them.

"Look around and ask, who are these people taking care of? They are taking care of the everyday New Yorker in the hospital, in the nursing home and in-home care," Joseph said. "If you go on the subway in the early morning, [you'll see them] traveling from the Bronx to Brooklyn to take care of the patients in their homes, who don't have anybody else but the worker who does that job rain, storm, or shine." Joseph said that he believed the city's dramatic drop in murders over recent decades was linked to the influx of hundreds of thousands of undocumented New Yorkers whose lives are defined by faith, family, and work.

Indeed, before the pandemic upended New York City, murders went from 2,262 in 1990 down to 319 in 2019. In 2020 the city recorded 462 homicides amidst the once-in-a-century mass-death event that shuttered the courts and the economy. To bring that number truly alive, try and hold in your head what 2,000 pairs of shoes would look like, and then multiply that by many years of continued homicide declines before last year's spike. Each of those pairs of shoes is someone now living, who might otherwise have died violently.

The decline in burglaries was just as spectacular. There were 122,055 reported in 1990, and just 12,743 in 2020. Rapes were down by more than half, from 3,176 in 1990, to 1,415 in 2016. So much for Trump's doom and gloom about the scourge of living in a sanctuary city. This record decline in New York's violent crime — in the face of ever-growing diversity, with immigrants from all over the world — created a real estate market, before COVID struck, that transformed once crime-ridden neighborhoods into billion-dollar hot spots, attracting capital from around the planet.[117]

For New York City it has been the steady waves of both undocumented and documented immigrants that were central to the city's recovery since the 1970s fiscal crisis. David Dysseygaard Kallick, a senior fellow with the Fiscal Policy Institute, writes about the centrality of immigrants to New York City's success in a chapter in a book entitled *One Out of Three: Immigrant New York In The 21st Century*, edited by Nancy Foner.[118] "The increase in the number and proportion of immigrants in the city has fueled economic growth, filled in neighborhoods that had become underpopulated later during the 1970s, and helped make New York the extraordinarily diverse global city it is today, with immigrants working in a wide range of jobs from the top to the bottom of the economic ladder."

When I say that New York City welcomes undocumented immigrants, I don't mean some limp handshake from the Welcome Wagon with a free car-wash coupon. It is a full, unapologetic embrace; because the City understood that the struggle to be free and improve the circumstances of all of its children, no matter their origin, is the engine that has always powered progress. The City offers a municipal ID to help these folks prosper and take root, because it knows they are the heartbeat of an America that gets better with the arrival of every new family escaping some truly wounded part of the world.[119]

There was no more poignant display of New Yorkers' concern for the plight of immigrants than the spontaneous rallies organized by groups like Make the Road New York, at La Guardia Airport in June of 2018, to protest the Trump administration's policy of separating immigrant children from their parents, when it was learned some of those children were being sent to New York City. Similar protests were sparked by Trump's executive order banning travel to the United States from Muslim countries.

The contrast is stark: While capital has become increasingly mobile, capable of flying around the planet with just a keystroke to find the sanctuary that offers the least taxation and transparency, immigrant workers are often beaten and held at borders. Twenty years into the 21st century, technology and automation have further tipped the balance of power to capital, with the so-called gig economy, upending the long-standing social contract between employers and labor — and immigrants are caught in that vice.

This has played out dramatically on the streets of New York City amid fierce competition in the taxi industry with the advent of Uber and Lyft. In the late 1990s, long before ride-hailing companies caused the value of city taxi medallions to collapse, labor organizers Bhairavi Desai and Javaid Tariq formed the New York Taxi Workers Alliance. Today, it has 21,000 members from all over the world; and it has been successful at getting some regulatory relief for drivers, several of whom have died by suicide in recent years.

It's an effort that builds on the rich tradition of immigrant organizing that is part of the American union movement's DNA. "Going back to the Lawrence textile strike in 1912, you had two dozen different languages and vastly diverse political experiences at play," said Joshua Freeman. "And considering that the (New York Taxi Workers Alliance) membership is voluntary, it is impressive with how much they have accomplished."

The union's initial organizing drive started in 1996. "Since then, day and night, we struggled to organize the drivers," Tariq said. "It is a scattered labor force. It is not a factory, and there are people from over 100 countries with different languages." He continued, "We are out there in the summer, in the winter, in the snow going to the airports where the drivers are hanging out, to the change of shifts at the garages, to ethnic restaurants." Many members come from countries with authoritarian governments where protesting and labor organizing risk serious repercussions. Tariq said that driver engagement centers partly on civics. He said, "We are always telling them, 'You are in the USA. You are in America... You are a hardworking, law-abiding person, so you don't have to be afraid to speak up.' That's the main thing — if you don't speak up, people will crush you." And when one worker is so diminished, aren't we all?

Chapter 11: A Strong and Free Press

Throughout this book, one of the unifying themes has been how workers can obtain agency over their destiny by acting collectively. Workers put a lot at risk to form a union and are at a huge power disadvantage to do so, much like David facing off with Goliath. Armed only with their courage to stand up for a collective sense of right and wrong, they face multibillion-dollar corporate behemoths that are the very engine of the wealth concentration and radical income disparity that have come to define the global economy.

When news media professionals are represented by a union, they have an independent source of power that acts as the broader community's check on the hedge funds and multibillion-dollar corporations that increasingly own legacy news outlets. Journalists who gather local news for broadcast or publication are an essential part of the feedback loop for democracy, providing authenticated situational awareness that helps frame every debate. It also becomes "the first draft of history." It's how we know where we are in our narrative.

As destiny would have it, just weeks after Amazon used unethical (possibly unlawful) tactics to derail a union-organizing drive by warehouse workers in Bessemer, Alabama, journalists in northern New Jersey who work for the Gannett conglomerate became the latest in a long list of news outlets voting to form a union. The Gannett employees are affiliated with NorthJersey.com, *The Bergen Record*, the *Daily Record* and the *New Jersey Herald*.

The Gannett vote to unionize came less than a month after journalists at the *New York Daily News* voted 55 to 3 to join the NewsGuild of New York.[120] The news was reported in New York City's "hometown" newspaper in a story about the size of a birth announcement. But the fledgling union got in its two cents. "Our newsroom overwhelmingly voted to form this union after more than a year of organizing," the new union stated.

Tribune Publishing, a corporate behemoth like Gannett, owns the *Daily News*. In a poignant May 5, 2021, op-ed entitled "Please buy this newspaper: A Daily News reporter begs a local owner to rescue the tabloid from Alden Global Capital," veteran reporter Larry McShane recounted how Tribune "fired half the newsroom on a single morning in 2018… Tribune now plans to peddle the paper to Alden Global Capital, the notorious hedge fund known for decimating newspapers like *the Denver Post* before picking the bones for profit," wrote McShane, who was cheering for Stewart Bainum, "a Baltimore hotel magnate," to draw "fellow deep-pocketed investors" to help beat Alden's $630 million offer.[121] Ultimately, though, Alden Global Capital prevailed.

But other unionization efforts succeeded. Just two weeks before the *Daily News* journalists took their courageous step, a majority of the 650 *New York Times* tech workforce had voted to also join the NewsGuild, which already represented the 1,300 employees in the *Times* editorial workforce and business staff.[122]

So, why is the labor tide rising in America's newsrooms? As multiple economic studies have documented, since the 1970s, workers have seen their wages flatline or decline, even as technological developments grew their productivity to generate exponential growth in wealth as a result of the profits their labor had generated.[123]

Nowhere is this more evident than in the newspaper business, which I entered about 40 years ago through the loading dock door at *The Ridgewood News* in Bergen County, New Jersey. I started in the typesetting and composition department before making my way into the reporting staff by covering local zoning meetings. Over my decades as a reporter, I have watched as technology reduced the number of people required to produce the newspaper, but those labor savings never found their way into the paychecks of those of us who continued to do the actual work. Instead, it went to the capital interests that swallowed up local newspapers, paving the way for Wall Street to swallow up most of the entire industry.

We were told we were lucky to have jobs, a mantra that has only gotten louder as the corporate titans like Gannett, which now owns one in five of America's newspapers,[124] has gutted the staffs of the local newspapers it has devoured in an unrelenting squeeze play that puts profits over people.[125] "Since 2016, we have seen more than half of our colleagues lose their jobs, with cuts of over 250 people at *The Record*, the *Daily Record* and the *NJ Herald*," wrote the Gannett employees seeking union representation in their mission statement. "Staffers who were unceremoniously laid off include a reporter nearly nine months pregnant and a 30-year-veteran reporter who was forced to take a buyout after missing a single email to opt out of the process."

Their statement continued, "By forming a union, we are taking a stand for respect and dignity, and greater protections against unjust terminations and reductions in force. We are uniting with NewsGuild members around the country in a movement to save local news and ensure a seat at the table, when decisions are made that affect our paper and the news coverage we provide.[126] There is no journalism without journalists."

Gannett is hardly alone. According to the Pew Research Center's analysis, US newspapers "have shed half of their newsroom employees since 2008... From 2008 to 2019, overall newsroom employment in the U.S. dropped by 23%, according to the new analysis," Pew reported.[127] "In 2008, there were about 114,000 newsroom employees — reporters, editors, photographers and videographers — in five industries that produce news: newspaper,[128] radio,[129] broadcast television,[130] cable[131] and 'other information services' (the best match[132] for digital-native[133] news publishers). By 2019, that number had declined to about 88,000, a loss of about 27,000 jobs."

Where once there were local reporters covering local town halls and doing the shoe-leather work of visiting local police stations to check out the blotter each day, all too often we now just have local authorities using Facebook or Twitter to get their stories out to the public, without any independent vetting for accuracy. Should our local reporting be left entirely to interested bystanders — like 17-year-old like Darnella Frazier, who stood her ground and captured the murder in broad daylight of George Floyd — to hold local law enforcement accountable?

According to the Center for Information, Technology and Public Life at the University of North Carolina (CITAP), as a result of this "extinction level threat to local newspapers... more than one-fourth of the country's newspapers have disappeared, leaving residents in thousands of communities living in vast news deserts."[134] As a result — according to CITAP's analysis — in our country, "200 counties do not have a local newspaper, nearly 50% of counties only have one newspaper, usually a weekly, and more than 6% of counties have no dedicated news coverage at all" while "digital startups are focused on population-dense communities, rather than the rural areas most often abandoned by local newspapers."

This "extinction-level" threat to local reporting has civic and even civil-defense consequences, as we saw when thousands of violent protestors — armed with unvetted, but profitable conspiracy theories — nearly upended the peaceful transition of power for the first time in our nation's history and carried the Confederate "Stars and Bars" flag through the corridors of our Capitol. "Local news outlets play an important role in informing community members about local government, elections, and other civic events," CITAP concludes. "They also help to shape community views around common values and beliefs, creating a sense of shared purpose that can be a powerful uniting force within a town or county. Without a source for local news, community members get most of their news from social media, leaving them vulnerable to mis- and disinformation and exacerbating political polarization." And what fills in that "vacuum left by the disappearance of local news sources" is "information sources that are incomplete" and "may be misleading or deceptive."

With the contraction of authentically reported local news, what has filled the void has been social media clickbait and propaganda, as the nation lost the vital sense of situational awareness that comes from a vibrant local press. As I have chronicled in this book, the continued deterioration of neighborhoods in urban and rural America was largely missed through the Obama presidency, giving Trump the fertile soil of grievance in which to plant his anti-immigrant and white-supremacist animus. It's not hard to track the devolution of our national circumstance to the January 6th insurrection. Thousands were ready to overthrow our democracy because, in their own cyber-bubble, they were convinced that the 2020 election had been "stolen." After all, they heard it on the "news."

At their root, our nation's tragically fractured response to COVID and the fatal insurrection on January 6th are both killer weeds sprung from the same root stock. The increasing concentration of corporate ownership has not just wreaked havoc on the nation's news-gathering workforce, it has distorted every other industry. These trends only accelerated since the early 1980s, when President Reagan fired more than 11,000 air traffic controllers after they had gone on strike and banned them from federal employment for life. A similar scorched-earth approach gained traction with private employers who adopted his tactics.

Before Reagan's mass firing, close to one in four Americans had been represented by a union. In 2020, according to the Bureau of Labor Statistics, just 10.8 percent are (which is actually a 0.5 percent increase from the prior year).[135] In transportation, where the sizes of crews on trains and ships have been slashed, the results have been calamitous for people and the planet. Consider the 2014 runaway oil train that was unattended when it leveled a Quebec community's downtown, killing 47 residents.[136] And maritime fatigue, as a result of short staffing, has produced oil spills visible from space.[137] In the healthcare sector, we see it in the business model of nursing homes, where profiteers pay as little as they can to as few staff as possible to care for our most vulnerable. More than a year into the COVID pandemic, we have seen the consequences of that business model carried on the backs of low-wage caregivers, who have often had to work in more than one facility to make ends meet, sometimes spreading the deadly virus in the process.[138]

At both the state and federal level, our democracy has become captive to capital interests that have successfully pressed for deregulation in a world in which corporations can drive maximum profits with little accountability for social and environmental impacts, all subsidized by tax policy. Meanwhile, workers are blocked at every turn from organizing collectively in their own and their community's self-interest. And what has this brave new world dominated by Goliaths like Amazon and Gannett given us? According to Forbes, in October 2020, the U.S. Federal Reserve found that the top one percent of Americans had a combined net worth of $34.2 trillion in wealth — or 30.4 percent of all US household wealth — while the bottom 50 percent of the population held just $2.1 trillion, equivalent to 1.9 percent of all wealth.[139]

Is it merely coincidental that the breathtaking concentration of corporate media power that Gannett represents comes as the well-documented concentration of wealth continues to grow, even accelerating during the pandemic? With the historical decline of unions, there's been an explosion in so-called gig workers, who as "independent contractors" are part of a precarious workforce that lacks the basic safety net of employer-subsidized healthcare or access to workers' compensation in the event they are injured or disabled while working. No doubt, they too are told they are lucky to have a job, even if they can't really call it that.

This trend has been particularly pronounced in both the profit and nonprofit news-gathering organizations I have worked in. I went to work at CBS News' *MoneyWatch* as a gig worker in the summer of 2015, near the end of the second Obama term, at the network's headquarters on West 57th Street in New York City. It was at that job that my paths crossed with Sean Spicer, who would go on to become President Trump's White House spokesman. Before Spicer became a national treasure, though, he was my cartoon nemesis.

Over the years, I had written critically about the corporate news media, including CBS, but there was something really gratifying about having a CBS ID and walking the halls that had been graced by Edward R. Murrow and Walter Cronkite. True, I was not technically an employee, since CBS paid me through a temp agency, somewhat ironically called ZeroChaos. Once you're in your 60s in this America, you're grateful for every new line in your résumé. The gig paid $45 an hour, but I was in the mix of it, walking by the "CBS Evening News" set and other star-chamber settings.

I liked my colleagues at *MoneyWatch*. They were smart and had internalized a sort of gallows humor that I'd come to learn was fairly common in many corporate settings. Since the corporate workplace could be so capricious and arbitrary, you could be fired by the time you came back from lunch. You always did your best because, well, each day could be your last. Ironically, I was able to write about controversial topics, such as offshore money laundering under the provocative headline, "Is Delaware Home to a Grand Corruption?"[140] Back in 2013, exploring that same realm at WNYC, the public radio station where I had worked for more than a decade, such a story meant having to do battle in line-by-line script edits with the station's lawyer, lest we appear anti-business.[141]

At CBS, at least with my editors, there was no requirement to pull back on chronicling the ravages of debt-vulture global capitalism. For example, I had carte blanche to compare what debt was doing to both Greece and Puerto Rico, under the headline, "In Greece and Puerto Rico, the Rot Has a Similar Stench."[142] I wrote, "The outcomes, too, show a remarkable — and devastating — similarity. Some 44 percent of Greeks live below the poverty line today; in Puerto Rico, the figure is 45 percent. In both places, the backdrop is a battered labor market that leaves little opportunity for younger people."

Where I ran into trouble, back in November 2015, was when I suggested to my CBS editors that we do a story about how the rise of Donald Trump and Dr. Ben Carson via social media and grassroots fundraising — as well as the swelling tsunami of independent right-wing money — was loosening the Republican National Committee's (RNC) control of the party's brand.

The story was reviewed and posted on the website; but in a matter of hours, I got a call from my editor saying that the people running CBS News' Washington coverage were furious about the story and that I needed to call the top press guy for the RNC — Sean Spicer — and do some damage control. As has been my practice for more than four decades now, I had sought comment on the story before I filed it. In this case, I had even sent the RNC my transcript of what I had taken down after speaking with the press person who had been tasked to respond to my request for comment. (I was prepared to remind Spicer of this when I called.)

When I got through to Spicer, he just started berating me, saying that I wasn't a journalist and that I didn't know anything about politics. Most damning of all, apparently, was that I had written for *Salon*, and he just didn't know how I "had ever gotten a job with CBS.... You just make this stuff up." I started to raise my voice to match his and try to get a word in edgewise, but at one point I simply said, "Mr. Spicer, we are both yelling. I am going to hang up now and call you later."

So I did just that. He was just as hostile later, basically telling me that it was too late for me; I was "done" because he was "coming for me" through CBS corporate. A couple of hours later, I was told — much to my editors' chagrin — that the powers within CBS had ordered that the story be taken down. There was no explanatory retraction; it was just deleted. For me, it was one of those heart-through-instep moments that you remember your whole life.

The only remnant of the story in cyberspace lives on in MuckRack.com's listings (an online compendium of journalists' work): "Just as the internet and social media have disrupted the business world from top to bottom, so are they shaking up the world of big-money politics. Exhibit A: The Republican National Committee's traditional business model is being upended, as radical change in tech meets radical change in politics."

After all, CBS had that RNC debate coming up in South Carolina in February 2016. A month before my story was published, in October 2015, Reince Priebus had cracked the whip to show the major media outlets who was boss when he punished NBC over how that network conducted its CNBC debate. You either adopted the RNC narrative, or you risked a multimillion-dollar loss in potential advertising revenues.

My CBS *MoneyWatch* story had started innocently enough: "For decades, the Republican National Committee's business model was that of a monopoly that exercised tight control over its brand. It was up to the RNC to define just what it meant to be a member in good standing of the Grand Old Party that had gotten its start in the 1850s." I referenced the CNBC/RNC debate fiasco, and I pointed out how the national RNC organization was increasingly at odds with its own candidates, noting that "since the emergence of the Tea Party, the dancing elephants don't want to do chorus work." (Come on, that's kind of funny.)

It was reasonable to ask whether the "confluence of an infusion of hundreds of millions of dollars from outside groups — after the *Citizens United* [Supreme Court decision] — along with social media, now makes it possible for candidates to leapfrog the central party committee and engage voters and donors directly." I had lots of facts: For example, in 2015-16, more than 6,200 political-action committees and independent expenditure groups pulled in close to $800 million at the time, bigfooting the major parties.

I included quotes from widely respected political-science and pollster academics. "The base of the party is angry at their own central organization," Patrick Murray, director of Monmouth University's Polling Institute, told me. "The RNC does not know it yet, but it is a dead organization walking," said Doug Muzzio, a professor of political science at Baruch College. "The nature of campaigning has changed so radically with social media. These are seismic shifts." I referenced a Gallup poll that found that just 25 percent of the voters surveyed identified themselves as Republican, the lowest percentage since Gallup started posing the question 25 years ago.

Even Allison Mitchell, from the RNC press office, had had a chance to weigh in when I wrote the story, countering that her party was a vibrant organization on the upswing, well positioned to help its nominee take the White House in 2016. "The enthusiasm in giving to the RNC has resulted in record-breaking totals almost every month," said Mitchell. "Look back at 2011 and now, and it's hard to believe how much improvement there has been."

I referenced the fiscal lifeline that Congress and President Barack Obama had thrown to both major parties by lifting the cap on individual donations to the RNC and DNC. Consequently, a contributor previously entitled to make a $33,400 donation to a party was allowed to give more than $300,000, spread over three accounts

143

dedicated to a party's legal costs, its headquarters construction, and the expenses of its national conventions.

My boss and his boss were both annoyed that their superiors had spiked the story under RNC pressure. They commissioned me to try again with something that might pass muster with the CBS Washington gatekeepers, who were always worried about preserving access. Okay, I thought, I'll find prominent Republicans and ask them if our thesis was wrong. Former New Jersey Governor Tom Kean told me that the post-*Citizens United* tsunami of special-interest money flowing into the crowded GOP primary was marginalizing the traditional role of the national party organization and its state committees. "The party organization, through its state and county party chairs, used to have a strong role in picking the nominee; and I think the big outside money has eroded that to a large degree," Kean said. "Now, if you're a candidate and you have to choose between attending an official party event and going to see a billionaire, you're going to pick the billionaire."

Consequently, the former governor (and co-chair of the 9/11 Commission) said that, in the 2016 Republican primary free-for-all, what had become clear was that the RNC had indeed lost its monopoly on defining its brand: "The candidates no longer look to the party, but to the billionaires who can fund their campaigns; and this is bad for democracy."

In my second try to get a version of the banned story posted, I cited a report, put out in March 2014, by the RNC as a post-election analysis of the "disappointing" 2012 election, written by its Growth and Opportunity Project. The report raised concerns that in the aftermath of the 2002 McCain-Feingold ban on political parties receiving "soft money" (unregulated campaign cash), the RNC was at risk of being marginalized as the flow of big political giving shifted to "non-party organizations." One of the five authors of the RNC's *Growth and Opportunity Project Report* was Ari Fleischer, former White House Press Secretary under President George W. Bush. Fleischer's analysis of the RNC's current predicament in the face of the influx of hundreds of millions in unregulated political spending echoed that of Governor Kean. "The political parties play a much smaller role in American politics than they did 10 or 20 years ago," Fleischer told

144

me. "Billionaires have gained power as the political parties have lost it."

Sad to say, though probably not surprising, the second take of my story never saw the light of day. Alas, just in time for Christmas 2015, CBS told me that my gig at West 57th Street was over, and that I could file some posts from home for a while — a sort of consolation prize. They told me my work just wasn't generating enough "clicks" to stay on long-term. I suppose that could be true, despite the statistics I had seen. While my CBS boss was giving that "wishing me well in my future endeavors" talk, all I could hear were Spicer's words in my head.

Throughout the campaign, Trump had commandeered the airwaves and social media to the point where *The New York Times* reported that, by March 2016, Trump had garnered close to $2 billion in unearned media coverage from outlets like CBS, based on research done by the firm Quant Media.[143] He was a TV personality and knew how to make himself the center of a story without spending a cent. For the other candidates, countering that would require spending billions to even come close to keeping pace with what Trump was handed by media corporations that saw his candidacy as priming the pump for a gusher of media spending. You could only get "equal time" on America's airwaves if you could afford to pay for it.

Oddly, in February 2016, then-CBS CEO Les Moonves had been quite transparent about the symbiotic relationship between CBS's bottom line and Trump. Speaking before a Morgan Stanley Technology, Media & Telecom Conference on February 29, 2016, Moonves told the audience that, while the Trump campaign "may not be good for America," it was "damn good for CBS. I've never seen anything like this, and this is going to be a very good year for us," he predicted. "Sorry. It's a terrible thing to say. But bring it on Donald, keep going."

Losing my CBS gig was a major blow. I could no longer afford to pay the premium for my family's health insurance, still in effect under

COBRA from my tenure at WNYC; so, we lost our healthcare coverage. It set the stage for me to start working overnight at the local ACME grocery store in pursuit of healthcare coverage, while maintaining my writing during the day for *Salon*, WBGO[144], *City & State*[145] and *WhoWhatWhy.*[146] It was sort of my version of Barbara Ehrenreich's *Nickel and Dimed: On (Not) Getting by in America.*[147]

The group of men I worked with overnight at ACME were all making $25 an hour with platinum healthcare; and they had multiple weeks of paid vacation that they could rarely take, because, at the $9.13-an-hour rate (without healthcare coverage) that the store paid new hires for night crew, they couldn't find anyone to fill in.

These guys all looked like ex-bikers who were close to my age. They talked about how they knew they were the last of a disappearing group of men that made a living wage for manual labor and how much corporations were sucking the lifeblood out of America under both parties. They told me that no matter how many hours I worked, I would never get the brass ring of healthcare coverage, because management didn't want full-time employees driving up costs. Management would schedule part-timers just as close as they could to the weekly hour limit for "part-time" work, without crossing that line. We laughed at the way the robots out at the central warehouse in Pennsylvania had packed the massive grocery skids when they arrived. We were convinced they were plotting to take us out, when the robots would plant a 60-pound carton of kitty litter in a way that, once you cut the shrink-wrap binding the load together, the kitty litter would hit you on the head.

I wrote about the single mothers who worked at ACME and about their struggles to make ends meet; they were going to vote for Trump. Some people close to me said it would be a career-killer to write about my experiences in the grocery store, because it was a sign that I had failed at being a professional journalist. I pressed forward, though, transcribing interviews with union members who subscribed to Trump's anti-immigrant worldview as a way to explain their own diminished earning power. I held on to my belief that I had a feel for the real pulse of how the country was feeling, as the experiences and perspectives of my early life were brought current by working on the loading dock in the middle of the night and reporting during the day.

In April 2016, after I wrote my *Salon* story on how Michael Savage, the radio talk show host, was actually the "Godfather of Trumpism," I heard Savage read it word-for-word over the radio during his national broadcast for a couple of days.[148] It was surreal. Savage had assumed that I was a closet Trump supporter, because I had accurately reported on the systemic corruption of both major parties and their selling out of American interests to corporate and foreign agendas. (I had merely done my homework and pieced together my analysis from decades of investigative reporting.) There was no way to reach Savage, other than yelling back at the radio.

When it came time for the national political conventions that summer, I had enough freelance assignments — and free places to stay in Philadelphia[149] and Cleveland[150] — to make it worthwhile to cover the conventions. I figured I would just give my notice at ACME. After all, I had covered every convention since 2000; and if I worked nonstop for those two weeks, I could make serious money. It felt like flying without a net, with no healthcare coverage, especially since I had witnessed some intense street violence over the years at previous conventions. My ACME manager didn't accept my notice, though; he said, "come back when you're done." I did come back for a while, so the guys could get some of their vacations in; and then I got a full-time job writing for the Manhattan-based *Chief-Leader*, a publication that has covered public unions and the civil service since 1897. As it turned out, my time working at ACME was critical to my understanding the 2016 campaign and the alienation of the segment of the electorate that would opt for Trump's violent chaos.

Increasingly, the battle between global capital and labor is playing out in America's newsrooms, where journalists are forming unions as the way to gain agency over their work and to preserve the function of authentic local news-gathering that puts people first. We have seen what happens when the nation loses that kind of situational awareness of the places in which we live.

Epilogue

The task before is daunting, but there is ample evidence that we are up to it. When we act in our collective interest, we improve the circumstances of our families and communities — merely by trying. In organizing where we live and where we work, for the world we want, we counter the fear upon which corporative capitalism feeds. There's a powerful cohesion that comes from those conversations that stake out our common ground. What appears as an obstacle to us, as individuals, may be easily overcome collectively.

The impact of such reclaimed agency can't be overstated. It empowers those who dare to claim it. It has always been the perquisite for any revolutionary project that expands what we mean when we say, "We the People." We live in a time when the corporate media complex's profit model runs on analytics driven by micro-targeting that divides us and reduces us to the sum of our consumer transactions.

Yet, in the year since George Floyd's murder, a massive social movement has risen up organically and forced a national conversation that has already prompted state legislatures — and even Congress — to take up police-accountability legislation that had been languishing for a generation. Shepherding these bills through to enactment, though, is only part of what will be required to transform our notions of "public safety" into a more holistic system of "community well-being."

The ripple effects include gestures like President Biden's decision to travel to Tulsa, Oklahoma, on the Memorial Day Weekend 2021, to commemorate the 100th anniversary of the white-supremacist massacre that killed hundreds of African Americans and leveled a section of that city, which had come to be known as Black Wall Street for its prosperity.

Joe Wilson, noted labor historian and educator, said of Biden's visit, "It is historical and monumental—it is a seismic shift even compared to Obama. It sets the stage for follow-on legislation at the local, state, and federal levels in terms of equity and reparations — local communities being responsible, local companies being responsible. It sets the stage for a grassroots movement for reparations on a national level."

And, as we have seen with the successful campaigns of Representative Alexandria Ocasio-Cortez, Senator Bernie Sanders, and dozens of other progressive candidates, the power of social media and organizing grassroots movements can be harnessed to raise millions of dollars that can counter the corrupting influence of corporate dark money. It is possible, as the transport sector unions demonstrated amidst the pandemic's grounding of the nation's aviation industry, to use the power of organized labor to negotiate a multibillion-dollar government program that uplifts a workforce, while safeguarding taxpayers from the money being pocketed by CEOs and Wall Street.

In New York State, collaborating community-based activists, immigrant-rights groups, and labor unions were able to convince the legislature to raise taxes on the wealthiest by billions, while creating the first-in-the-nation unemployment program for the state's undocumented workers who'd lost their jobs during the pandemic. The same coalition secured passage of the New York Health and Essential Rights (HERO) Act, which granted workplace protections from airborne viruses like COVID for private sector workers and empowered employees — regardless of whether they were in a union — to organize workplace committees to address workplace safety issues.

We do not have to accept streetscapes pockmarked with zombie and derelict homes wasting in waiting, while homeless families drag their possessions from temporary shelter to derelict motel. As recounted in the book *The Land Bank Revolution: How Ohio's Communities Fought Back Against the Foreclosure Crisis*, by Jim Rokakis and Gus Frangos, community-housing activists worked with engaged local officials to

150

raise hundreds of millions of dollars to demolish tens of thousands of "derelict structures" and in the process "made life better for countless Ohioans."[151]

Decades of elected officials acting only in the service of corporations that put profits over people require that we undertake a dynamic realignment that elevates the needs and concerns of the general population above those of the privileged few who rent our political system. The complex issues we face that have our country stuck require thinking big and using collective strategies across interest groups by finding where our agendas intersect. Sadly, all too often the solutions that emerge out of the *status quo* are too small-bore to address the problems at hand, which only grow in dimension with our half measures. We are too often content with symbolic efforts, rather than the radical changes our circumstances require.

In March 2021, New York City Mayor Bill de Blasio announced that the city was going to name a new Staten Island Ferry for Dorothy Day, the radical activist-journalist and co-founder of the Catholic Worker Movement, who died in 1990.[152] Day, a devout Catholic, was a committed pacifist, as well as a lifelong advocate for the poor and for workers' rights. (Incidentally, she was among those who was jailed picketing President Wilson's White House for women's suffrage.) It was another symbolic gesture that references a radical person — without being a radical action — and keeps the oppressive architecture in place.

"I do not see why we must accept the inevitability of war," wrote Day. "It was only in the last century that slavery was done away with here in this country, and I suppose that everybody thought it was inevitable, something to be accepted before that time. If we are working toward peace, we must look with hope that in a future generation we will do away with war."

"We need to change the system," Day wrote on another occasion. "We need to overthrow, not the government, as the authorities are always accusing the Communists of conspiring to teach to do, but this rotten, decadent, putrid industrial capitalist system which breeds such suffering in the white sepulcher of New York."

What if instead of just attaching Day's name to a new Staten Island Ferry — which provides free passage to tens of thousands of essential workers every day — we used the occasion to also declare that all mass transit would be free for all, as part of a new ordering of things that puts working people first?

As the nation emerges from the COVID pandemic, we can't let workers lose the leverage they gained when the corporate news referred to them as "essential." After decades of wages flatlining or dropping, there's evidence that the balance of power between capital and labor may be tipping ever so slightly towards labor. Only an organized and militant workforce can build on these ephemeral gains, which still don't make up for the decades of lost wage gains.

All too often, news reporting on the political economy internalizes the worldview of the employers and the owners. In 24 states where the Republicans control the state legislature, they are cutting off the additional $300 a week in the federally funded supplement to unemployment benefits as a way of taking the pressure off low-wage employers to raise wages and improve benefits to induce workers off the sidelines.

In the many months of the pandemic, we saw thousands of workers die from COVID, and we can expect millions more to have to deal with long-term health consequences from their time serving others. It's not an overstatement to say that we are seeing a recalibration of the risks and benefits of work. Whenever the forces of competition, due to a tight labor market, seem to tip slightly to the benefit of workers — in terms of higher pay and improved benefits — the corporate news media sound the alarm that labor is "getting over" and taking advantage of the owners. This anti-worker bias manifests itself when news outlets suggest it's scandalous that any worker, be it a stagehand, transit worker, or firefighter, could make a six-figure salary; while the same outlets heap praise on the industry and brilliance of any member of the billionaire class.

And as the dire images of death and loss that defined the pandemic fade, there will be the push to forget the degree to which our existing and deepening race-based economic disparities consigned so many to a premature and painful departure from this earthly plain. The only way to counteract this corporatist push to pick up where we left

152

off — with workers being underpaid and exploited — is to hold the system accountable for what was an avoidable death toll from a pandemic that had been predicted for years by public health experts. From now forward, each year that goes by without universal health care lays the groundwork for yet another mass-death pandemic event — and we will likely be told again that "nobody saw it coming."

But there's no doubt that if you've made it this far in my diagnosis of what's got us stuck as a nation, you too have a sense of the scale of change that's required to move us forward. Once we fully process what that means, the only thing left for us to do is take action.

Acknowledgements

The book would not have been published without the essential help from my wife Debra Sabatini Hennelly, Democracy at Work's Liz Phillips and the meticulous copy editing by Marilou Baughman.

With the assistance of Richard Wolff, through my appearances on his program Economic Update, which were produced by Maria Carnemolla, I focused my analysis in preparation for this project.

Throughout the pandemic, the friendship via Zoom that Debbie and I found with Rick Wolff and Dr. Harriet Fraad was a great support and comfort.

I owe much to the small army of people who, over the years, trusted me to tell their stories, like Lt. Angela Shirlaw, the New York State Court officer who used her own struggles for 9/11 WTC benefits as a way to empower her colleagues to do the same. It was by covering the disability battles of former FDNY Paramedic Gary Smiley and others that I got a feel for just what 9/11 WTC survivors could be put through by an abusive bureaucracy.

Much of the reporting for this book was accomplished over a decade while I worked at WNYC, WBGO, the Chief-Leader, Salon, City & State and Insider NJ.

My relationship with WBGO, 88.3 FM, Newark NJ's essential jazz station, goes back many years and my colleagues Doug Doyle and Steve Williams have always been supportive of my efforts to tell some of the stories in this volume.

Similarly, my editors at Salon, Andrew O'Hehir and Keith Spencer, provided me with a national platform to tell the under-reported stories about the essential American workforce, which has been undervalued my entire adult life.

During my tenure at WNYC, I was edited by Kaari Pitkin, Karen Frillmann, Patricia Willens, Julianne Welby, and Nancy Solomon, and online by Xana O'Neill. I benefited from the production support of Janna Flanagan and Richard Yeh.

At Insider NJ, my editor Max Pizarro, and the site's owner, John Graham, have encouraged my work. At City & State, my editor Jon Lentz and Tom Allon, the site's publisher, supported my long format investigative journalism.

My work at the Chief-Leader has been edited by Richard Steier, whose knowledge of all things New York City civil service is legendary.

I could not have continued pressing on with journalism all these years without the support and insights from editors who became dear friends like Dan Bischoff, with whom I worked at the Village Voice, and Lorraine Ash, who I encountered at the Ridgewood News a few decades ago and have been talking with ever since.

Much of my network has its foundations at Ramapo College, which I attended in the 1970s and where I worked as an adjunct teaching environmental journalism. When I was there, Murray Bookchin and Joe Johnson, who have both left this world, were mentors. In the years since, I have come to rely on Dr. Michael Edelstein for his big picture analysis.

My paths first crossed with Adele M. Stan when she was the editor of Ramapo College's newspaper and we were both students. In the decades since, we continued to track America's essential story. She edited my 2016 Cornel West interview for Alternet, which is excerpted in this book.

A number of people in the labor movement have supported my work at pivotal points when their help was critical. That list includes Al Hagan, Arthur Cheliotes, Andy Stern, Barbara Edmonds, Henry Garrido, Wanda Williams, and the late Oliver Gray.

I want to thank John Fugelsang, Leonard Lopate, Arne Arnesen, John Kane, and Michael G. Haskins for providing me regular opportunities on their radio programs to extemporaneously discuss the tick-tock of our pandemic / insurrection era.

I would be remiss if I did not thank Brian Reddy, Joel Kupferman, Noreen Staples, Nelson Flores, Peter Woolley, and James Henry for their support and friendship.

A day doesn't go by that I don't miss A.J. Woolston-Smith, my dear friend and fellow seeker of the truth, who served in British intelligence during WWII. During his American phase, when he did his best to keep the "colonies" honest, he helped me track organized crime and political corruption in the Hudson Valley, New York City, and the environs of New Jersey.

I am grateful for the love and support of my wife Debbie, my daughters, Emily Hennelly McCollum, Abigail Hennelly and Rebecca Hennelly, as well as my in-laws Frank Sabatini and Dr. Sandra Sabatini.

About the Author

Bob Hennelly is an award-winning print and broadcast journalist. He is currently the City Hall reporter for *The Chief-Leader*, a New-York-City-based newspaper that has been covering public unions since 1897, and private-sector unions since 2017. He is also a regular contributor to *Salon*, *Insider NJ*, and WBGO-Newark Public Radio. Prior to joining *The Chief* in 2016, he covered the global economy for *CBS MoneyWatch*.

From 2003 until 2013, he was a senior reporter for WNYC-New York Public Radio, where he also was a National Public Radio contributor. Prior to WNYC, he served as a national correspondent for Pacifica Network News. Prior to Pacifica, he was on staff at *The Village Voice*.

He has been a freelance reporter for CBS's "60 Minutes" and in New Jersey for *The New York Times*. His writing has also been published by *The Detroit Free Press*, *The Miami Herald*, *The Christian Science Monitor*, *The Bergen Record*, and *The Guardian*. His work has also been featured on *Alternet*, *Raw Story*, *Portside* and *Real Clear Politics*.

He lives with his wife, Debbie, and their two rescue dogs at the New Jersey Shore.

About Democracy at Work

Democracy at Work is a non-profit 501(c)3 that produces media and live events. Based on the book Democracy at Work: A Cure for Capitalism by Richard D. Wolff, our work analyzes capitalism critically as a systemic problem and advocates for democratizing workplaces as part of a systemic solution. We seek a stronger, fuller democracy – in our politics and culture as well as in our economy – based on workers' equal collaboration and shared leadership inside enterprises and throughout society.

Democracy at Work produces the shows *Economic Update with Richard D. Wolff*, *Global Capitalism Live Economic Update*, *David Harvey's Anti-Capitalist Chronicles*, *Capitalism Hits Home*, *All Things Co-op*, and *Cities After...*

Democracy at Work has also published the books *The Sickness is the System: When Capitalism Fails to Save Us from Pandemics or Itself* (2020), *Understanding Socialism* (2019) and *Understanding Marxism* (2018), all authored by Richard D. Wolff.

Each of these is a collaborative effort, and are brought to you by the hard work and dedication of a small team of workers. To keep costs low, we work via a digital office and rely on donated time from Prof. Wolff as well as other volunteer contributors. We are a nonprofit but do our best to operate internally as a cooperative to better embody the ideals we believe are a critical part of effective system change.

Learn more: **www.democracyatwork.info**

Notes

[1] BBC News. (2016). *Foxconn replaces '60,000 factory workers with robots.'* Retrieved from https://www.bbc.com/news/technology-36376966

[2] BBC News. (2015). *Will a robot take your job?* Retrieved from https://www.bbc.com/news/technology-34066941

[3] Fox Business. (2017). *Fmr. McDonald's USA CEO: $35K Robots Cheaper Than Hiring at $15 Per Hour.* Retrieved from https://www.foxbusiness.com/features/fmr-mcdonalds-usa-ceo-35k-robots-cheaper-than-hiring-at-15-per-hour

[4] CBS News. (2016). *Undocumented own U.S. homes, pay billions in taxes.* Retrieved from https://www.cbsnews.com/news/undocumented-own-u-s-homes-and-pay-billions-in-taxes/

[5] Fair Share Housing Center. (n.d.) *What is the Mount Laurel Doctrine?* Retrieved from https://fairsharehousing.org/mount-laurel-doctrine/

[6] PBS. (2017). *NJ's Affordable Housing Crisis: How Did We Get Here?* Retrieved from https://www.pbs.org/wnet/chasing-the-dream/stories/njs-affordable-housing-crisis-get/

[7] NJ Spotlight News. (2017). *New Jersey Still Bogged Down in Foreclosures While Rest of Country Recovering.* Retrieved from https://www.njspotlight.com/2017/01/17-01-25-new-jersey-is-still-bogged-down-in-foreclosures-while-rest-of-country-recovers/

[8] Rutgers School of Law. (2015). *I/M/O Adoption of N.J.A.C. 5:96 and 5:97 by The New Jersey Council on Affordable Housing.* Retrieved from http://165.230.71.5/query.php?var=M-392-14

[9] NJ.com. (2019). *N.J. leads the nation in foreclosures.* Retrieved from https://www.nj.com/data/2018/01/foreclosure_rates_in_all_21_counties_rankeddddddd.html

[10] USA Today. (2021). *Capitol riot arrests: See who's been charged across the U.S.* Retrieved from https://eu.usatoday.com/storytelling/capitol-riot-mob-arrests/

[11] Insider NJ. (2021). *D.C. the Morning After: The Smoke has Cleared but the Danger hasn't.* Retrieved from https://www.insidernj.com/d-c-morning-smoke-cleared-danger-hasnt/

[12] MSNBC. (2021). *Lt. General Honoré calls for investigation of 'complicit' defense in Capitol building insurrection.* Retrieved from https://www.bing.com/videos/search?q=general+honoree+trump+capitol+complicity&docid=13829838614404&mid=C5C749FFB7C78C08A30CC5C749FFB7C78C08A30C&view=detail&FORM=VIRE

[13] Governor's Select Commission on Civil Disorder, State of New Jersey (1968). *Report for Action.* Retrieved from https://www.ojp.gov/pdffiles1/Digitization/69748NCJRS.pdf

[14] The New York Times. (2017). *Five Days of Unrest That Shaped, and Haunted, Newark.* Retrieved from https://www.nytimes.com/2017/07/11/nyregion/newark-riots-50-years.html

[15] Mother Jones. (2007). *Newark to New Orleans: The Myth of the Black Sniper.* Retrieved from https://www.motherjones.com/politics/2007/07/newark-new-orleans-myth-black-sniper/

[16] History Matters. (n.d.) *"The Communications Media, Ironically, Have Failed to Communicate": The Kerner Report Assesses Media Coverage of Riots and Race Relations.* Retrieved from http://historymatters.gmu.edu/d/6553

[17] Salon. (2020). *COVID explodes in Newark: Tragic result of a long legacy of urban abuse and neglect.* Retrieved from I/M/O Adoption of N.J.A.C. 5:96 and 5:97 by The New Jersey Council on Affordable Housing

[18] Nurse Practitioner Healthcare Foundation and New Jersey Health Care Quality Institute. (2016). *Feasibility Study of Newark, New Jersey.* Retrieved from https://www.nphealthcarefoundation.org/media/filer_public/2f/fe/2ffe9274-8849-4412-ac09-26e1cf534712/newark_feasibility_complete_report_7_10_2016.pdf

[19] American Society of Civil Engineers. (n.d.). *Report Card for America's Infrastructure.* Retrieved from https://infrastructurereportcard.org/making-the-grade/

[20] Natural Resources Defense Council. (2017). *Newark's Lead in Drinking Water Contamination Recalls Flint Crisis; Local and National Groups Challenge Officials for a Stronger Response.* Retrieved from https://www.nrdc.org/media/2017/170921

[21] Centers for Disease Control and Prevention. (n.d.). *Childhood Lead Poisoning Prevention.* Retrieved from https://www.cdc.gov/nceh/lead/default.htm

[22] Du Bois Review. (2016). *The Racial Ecology of Lead Poisoning.* Retrieved from https://scholar.harvard.edu/files/alixwinter/files/sampson_winter_2016.pdf

23 Scientific American. (2016). *Thousands of U.S. Areas Afflicted with Lead Poisoning beyond Flint's*. Retrieved from https://www.scientificamerican.com/article/thousands-of-u-s-areas-afflicted-with-lead-poisoning-beyond-flints/

24 Health Affairs. (2017). *Contaminated Childhood: The Chronic Lead Poisoning of Low-Income Children and Communities of Color in the United States*. Retrieved from https://www.healthaffairs.org/do/10.1377/hblog20170808.061398/full/

25 American Academy of Pediatrics. (2016). *Prevention of Childhood Lead Toxicity*. Retrieved from https://pediatrics.aappublications.org/content/pediatrics/138/1/e20161493.full.pdf

26 Reuters. (2017). *Corporate tax breaks cost U.S. schools billions of lost revenue: report*. Retrieved from https://www.reuters.com/article/us-usa-taxes-subsidies-education/corporate-tax-breaks-cost-u-s-schools-billions-of-lost-revenue-report-idUSKBN1O30B3

27 Fox Business. (2019). *Newark makes HQ2 pitch to Amazon after collapse of NYC deal*. Retrieved from https://www.foxbusiness.com/politics/newark-makes-hq2-pitch-to-amazon-after-collapse-of-nyc-deal

28 The New York Times. (2015). *Poll Finds Most in U.S. Hold Dim View of Race Relations*. Retrieved from https://www.nytimes.com/2015/07/24/us/poll-shows-most-americans-think-race-relations-are-bad.html?_r=0

29 Pitney Farm. (2019). *Pitney Farm House Razed*. Retrieved from https://pitneyfarm.org/2019/05/02/pitney-farm-house-razed/

30 Supreme Court of New Jersey. (1793). *State v. Pitney, 1 N.J. (Manumission) 31 (1793)*. Retrieved by https://cite.case.law/nj-manumission/1/31/6677197/

31 Unitarian Universalist Association. (n.d.). *What is the Doctrine of Discovery?* Retrieved from https://www.uua.org/racial-justice/dod/what-doctrine-discovery

32 Salon. (2019). *Reparations economics 101*. Retrieved from https://www.salon.com/2019/06/23/reparations-economics-101/

33 Unitarian Universalist Association. (n.d.). *What is the Doctrine of Discovery?* Retrieved from https://www.uua.org/racial-justice/dod/what-doctrine-discovery

34 NJ State Library. (n.d.) *Afro-Americans in New Jersey: a short history*. Giles R. Wright; Trenton, NJ, New Jersey Historical Commission, 1989. Retrieved by https://www.njstatelib.org/research_library/new_jersey_resources/highlights/afro-americans/

35 Tinton Falls New Jersey. (n.d.). *History*. Retrieved by https://www.tintonfalls.com/visitor/history

[36] Baltimore, The Johns Hopkins press (1896). *A study of slavery in New Jersey*. Retrieved from https://archive.org/details/studyslavery00coolrich

[37] David Mitros. *Jacob Green and the Slavery Debate in Revolutionary Morris County, New Jersey* (Morris County Heritage Commission, 1993).

[38] David Mitros. *Slave Records of Morris County, New Jersey: 1756-1841* (Morris County Historical, 2002).

[39] History of American Women. (n.d.). *Slavery in New Jersey*. Retrieved from https://www.womenhistoryblog.com/2008/02/slavery-in-new-jersey.html

[40] James J. Gigantino II. *The Ragged Road to Abolition*. (University of Pennsylvania Press, 2016).

[41] Office of Inspector General. (2003). *EPA's Response to the World Trade Center Collapse: Challenges, Successes, and Areas for Improvement*. Retrieved from https://www.epa.gov/sites/production/files/2015-12/documents/wtc_report_20030821.pdf

[42] The Center for Public Integrity. (2008). *EPA Misleads on Air Quality After 9/11 Attacks*. Retrieved from https://publicintegrity.org/politics/epa-misleads-on-air-quality-after-9-11-attacks

[43] Union of Concerned Scientists. (2008). *World Trade Center Rescue Workers Believed EPA, Ended Up Sick*. Retrieved from https://www.ucsusa.org/resources/world-trade-center-rescue-workers-believed-epa-ended-sick

[44] The Guardian. (2016). *Former EPA head admits she was wrong to tell New Yorkers post-9/11 air was safe*. Retrieved from https://www.theguardian.com/us-news/2016/sep/10/epa-head-wrong-911-air-safe-new-york-christine-todd-whitman

[45] Representative Carolyn B. Maloney. (2007). *New WTC Registry Report Shows National Impact of 9/11 Health Crisis – Press Release*. Retrieved from https://maloney.house.gov/media-center/press-releases/new-wtc-registry-report-shows-national-impact-911-health-crisis

[46] BBC News. (2001). *Ground Zero fires finally out*. Retrieved from http://news.bbc.co.uk/2/hi/americas/1720423.stm

[47] The Chief-Leader. (2019). *Council WTC Bill Would Notify DOE Staff, Pupils*. Retrieved by https://thechiefleader.com/news/news_of_the_week/council-wtc-bill-would-notify-doe-staff-pupils/article_2c77ce6e-83ba-11e9-96c0-9bbf3205bf50.html

[48] The Chief-Leader. (2019). *WTC Health Program Director: Half Of 9/11 Firefighters Have Lung Issues*. Retrieved by https://thechiefleader.com/news/news_of_the_week/wtc-health-program-director-half-of-firefighters-have-lung-issues/article_ecaf7ab6-8d4b-11e9-afa7-b3f064a3d105.html

49 World Trade Center Health Program. (2021). *Advances in the Screening and Treatment for WTC Responders and Survivors - WD2813.* Retrieved from https://www.cdc.gov/wtc/training_advances_2.html

50 The Chief-Leader. (2018). *WTC 'Survivors' Have Tougher Rules on Aid.* Retrieved by https://thechiefleader.com/news/news_of_the_week/wtc-survivors-have-tougher-rules-on-aid/article_6710b404-dea7-11e8-9bb7-1b9a7eba1927.html

51 The Chief-Leader. (2021). *Postal Unions Hope House Probe Of USPS Virus Response Gets Answers.* Retrieved by https://thechiefleader.com/news/news_of_the_week/postal-unions-hope-house-probe-of-usps-virus-response-gets-answers/article_c853996a-76db-11eb-a0ee-0bc47da6b045.html

52 People. (2021). *Nearly One-Third of People with 'Mild' COVID-19 Cases Still Have 'Persistent Symptoms' Months Later: Study.* Retrieved from https://www.msn.com/en-us/health/medical/nearly-one-third-of-people-with-e2-80-98mild-e2-80-99-covid-19-cases-still-have-e2-80-98persistent-symptoms-e2-80-99-months-later-study/ar-BB1dUPEu?ocid=uxbndlbing

53 American Journal of Industrial Medicine. (2016). *Expecting the Unexpected: A Mixed Methods Study of Violence to EMS Responders in an Urban Fire Department.* Retrieved from https://onlinelibrary.wiley.com/doi/epdf/10.1002/ajim.22550

54 The Chief-Leader. (2017). *Veteran EMT Killed By Crazed Man Who Hit Her With Ambulance.* Retrieved by https://thechiefleader.com/news/news_of_the_week/veteran-emt-killed-by-crazed-man-who-hit-her-with/article_29e9eeb2-ff81-11e6-b1dd-ef63bdfec845.html

55 CNN. (2019). *Two Boston EMTs assaulted, one stabbed multiple times, by a patient.* Retrieved from https://amp.cnn.com/cnn/2019/07/11/us/boston-emt-stabbed-trnd/index.html

56 Body Armor News. (n.d.). *Body Armor to be Worn by EMTs Due to Increased Risk of Violence.* Retrieved by https://www.bodyarmornews.com/ems-bulletproof-vests/

57 Modern Healthcare. (2019). *Healthcare CEOs again lead the way in pay.* Retrieved from https://www.modernhealthcare.com/finance/healthcare-ceos-again-lead-way-pay

58 Bureau of Labor Statistics. (n.d). *EMTs and Paramedics.* Retrieved from https://www.bls.gov/ooh/healthcare/mobile/emts-and-paramedics.htm

59 Data USA. (2017). *Emergency Medical Technicians & Paramedics.* Retrieved from https://datausa.io/profile/soc/emergency-medical-technicians-paramedics

60 Society for Human Resource Management. (2018). *New California Law Requires Emergency Responders to Be on Call During Breaks.* Retrieved from https://www.shrm.org/resourcesandtools/legal-and-compliance/state-and-local-updates/pages/new-california-law-requires-emergency-responders-to-be-on-call-during-breaks.aspx

165

[61] Vigil NH, Grant AR, Perez O, Blust RN, Chikani V, Vadeboncoeur TF, Spaite DW, Bobrow BJ. *Death by Suicide-The EMS Profession Compared to the General Public.* (2019). Retrieved by https://pubmed.ncbi.nlm.nih.gov/30136908/

[62] Salon. (2019). *Chronically underpaid EMTs are being assaulted at record rates.* Retrieved by https://www.salon.com/2019/09/22/chronically-underpaid-emts-are-being-assaulted-at-record-rates/

[63] NBC News. (2019). *What if you call 911 and no one comes?* Retrieved by https://www.nbcnews.com/health/health-care/there-s-shortage-volunteer-ems-workers-ambulances-rural-america-n1068556

[64] Salon. (2020). *The COVID-19 outbreak has made universal healthcare into a national security issue.* Retrieved by https://www.salon.com/2020/03/08/the-covid-19-outbreak-has-made-universal-healthcare-into-a-national-security-issue/

[65] The Chief-Leader. (2020). *EMTs Quitting to Take Firefighter Jobs Causing Ambulance-Crew Shortages.* Retrieved by https://thechiefleader.com/news/news_of_the_week/emts-quitting-to-take-firefighter-jobs-causing-ambulance-crew-shortages/article_8633516a-43a6-11ea-8901-ef6274dab2ce.html

[66] David, G., & Brachet, T. (2009). *Retention, learning by doing, and performance in emergency medical services. Health services research, 44(3), 902–925.* Retrieved by https://doi.org/10.1111/j.1475-6773.2009.00953.x

[67] International Association of Firefighters. (n.d.). Retrieved by https://www.iaff.org/

[68] U.S. Fire Administration. (n.d.). Retrieved by https://www.usfa.fema.gov/about/index.html

[69] Upstander Project. (n.d.). Doctrine of Discovery. Retrieved by https://upstanderproject.org/firstlight/doctrine

[70] Michelle Alexander. The New Jim Crow: Mass Incarceration in the Age of Colorblindness. (The New Press, 2012).

[71] Remember the Triangle Fire Coalition. (n.d.). Retrieved by http://rememberthetrianglefire.org/

[72] Retail, Wholesale and Department Store Union. (n.d.). Retrieved by https://www.rwdsu.info/

[73] Supreme Court of the State of New York. (2021). *THE PEOPLE OF THE STATE OF NEW YORK by LETITIA JAMES, Attorney General of the State of New York, against AMAZON.COM INC., AMAZON.COM SALES, INC., and AMAZON.COM SERVICES LLC.* Retrieved by https://iapps.courts.state.ny.us/nyscef/ViewDocument?docIndex=muvelgaOEvSt6Yc1gGqzAg==

[74] The Chief-Leader. (2021). *New York Trails Jersey, 18 Other States In Virus Workers' Comp Protections*. Retrieved by https://thechiefleader.com/news/news_of_the_week/new-york-trails-jersey-18-other-states-in-virus-workers-comp-protections/article_16664a72-8833-11eb-911d-9b2ae8428441.html

[75] The Guardian. (2021). *Our key findings about US healthcare worker deaths in the pandemic's first year*. Retrieved by https://www.theguardian.com/us-news/ng-interactive/2020/dec/22/lost-on-the-frontline-our-findings-to-date

[76] National Law Enforcement Officers Memorial Fund. (2021). *NLEOMF Statement on Covid-19 and its Impact on Law Enforcement*. Retrieved by https://nleomf.org/memorial-fund-statement-on-covid-19-and-its-impact-on-law-enforcement

[77] National Priorities Project. (n.d.). Retrieved by https://www.nationalpriorities.org/

[78] National Priorities Project. (2021). *The Pentagon Increase Is the Size of the Entire CDC Budget*. Retrieved by https://www.nationalpriorities.org/blog/2021/05/14/pentagon-increase-size-entire-cdc-budget/

[79] OpenSecrets.org Center for Responsive Politics. (2019-2010). *Defense*. Retrieved by https://www.opensecrets.org/industries/indus.php?Ind=D

[80] *Citizens United v. Federal Election Commission*. (n.d.). Oyez. Retrieved June 24, 2021, from https://www.oyez.org/cases/2008/08-205

[81] Brennan Center for Justice. (2019). *Citizens United Explained*. Retrieved by https://www.brennancenter.org/our-work/research-reports/citizens-united-explained

[82] Brennan Center for Justice. (2015). *Citizens United Five Years Later*. Retrieved by https://www.brennancenter.org/our-work/research-reports/citizens-united-five-years-later

[83] Sheldon Whitehouse, Melanie Wachtell Stinnett. *Captured: The Corporate Infiltration of American Democracy*. (The New Press, 2017).

[84] Salon. (2021). *Officer Brian Sicknick was an Iraq vet who criticized Bush's war — and died defending democracy*. Retrieved by https://www.salon.com/2021/01/11/officer-brian-sicknick-was-an-iraq-vet-who-criticized-bushs-war--and-died-defending-democracy_partner/

[85] Brown University, Watson Institute, International & Public Affairs. (n.d). *Costs of War*. Retrieved by https://watson.brown.edu/costsofwar/

[86] AlterNet. (2016). *Cornel West: Trump Will Be a Neofascist Catastrophe and Clinton a Neoliberal Disaster*. Retrieved by https://www.alternet.org/2016/07/cornel-west-trump-will-be-neofascist-catastrophe-and-clinton-neoliberal-disaster/

[87] Investopedia. (2021). *Zombie Title.* Retrieved by
https://www.investopedia.com/terms/z/zombie-titles.asp

[88] National Association of Counties. (2016). *Priorities in American's Counties 2016 – A survey of County Officials.* Retrieved by https://www.naco.org/resources/priorities-americas-counties-2016-survey-county-officials

[89] Investopedia. (2021). *Quantitative Easing 2 – QE2.* Retrieved by
https://www.investopedia.com/terms/q/quantitative-easing-2-qe2.asp

[90] The New York Times. (2016). *The Crisis of Minority Unemployment.* Retrieved by
https://www.nytimes.com/2016/02/21/opinion/sunday/the-crisis-of-minority-unemployment.html

[91] U.S. Government Accountability Office. (2021). *Behavioral Health: Patient Access, Provider Claims Payment, and the Effect of the COVID-19 Pandemic.* Retrieved by
https://www.gao.gov/assets/gao-21-437r.pdf

[92] John M. Barry. *The Great Influenza: The Story of the Deadliest Pandemic in History.* (Penguin Books, 2005).

[93] Salon. (2020). *Trump tells governors seeking respirators and other medical equipment to try getting it themselves.* Retrieved by https://www.salon.com/2020/03/16/trump-tells-governors-seeking-respirators-and-other-medical-equipment-to-try-getting-it-themselves/

[94] Salon. (2020). *Cuomo tells Trump admin. to "pick the 26,000 people who are going to die" amid ventilator shortage.* Retrieved by https://www.salon.com/2020/03/24/cuomo-tells-trump-admin-to-pick-the-26000-people-who-are-going-to-die-amid-ventilator-shortage/

[95] Salon. (2020). *First responders suspect "crazy increase in cardiac deaths" in NYC is linked to COVID-19.* Retrieved by https://www.salon.com/2020/04/07/first-responders-suspect-crazy-increase-in-cardiac-deaths-in-nyc-is-linked-to-covid-19/

[96] Salon. (2020). *First responders suspect "crazy increase in cardiac deaths" in NYC is linked to COVID-19.* Retrieved by https://www.salon.com/2020/04/07/first-responders-suspect-crazy-increase-in-cardiac-deaths-in-nyc-is-linked-to-covid-19/

[97] Woolf SH, Chapman DA, Sabo RT, Zimmerman EB. *Excess Deaths From COVID-19 and Other Causes in the US, March 1, 2020, to January 2, 2021. JAMA.* 2021;325(17):1786-1789. doi:10.1001/jama.2021.5199

[98] Garber AM. *Learning From Excess Pandemic Deaths. JAMA.* 2021;325(17):1729-1730. doi:10.1001/jama.2021.5120

[99] The Washington Post. (2019). *Federal workers in Washington aren't the only ones going without pay.* Retrieved by https://www.washingtonpost.com/graphics/2019/politics/shutdown-federal-worker-impact/?utm_term=.f635eed789ec

[100] Federal Law Enforcement. (n.d.). *What is TSA?* Retrieved by https://www.federallawenforcement.org/tsa/

[101] NBC News. (2016). *NBC News Exit Poll in Ohio: State Looks to Trump on the Economy.* Retrieved by https://www.nbcnews.com/card/nbc-news-exit-poll-ohio-state-looks-trump-economy-n680531

[102] CBS News. (2016). *Getting closer to the roots of economic insecurity.* Retrieved by https://www.cbsnews.com/news/getting-closer-to-the-roots-of-economic-insecurity/

[103] Association of Flight Attendants. (2019). *Sara Nelson Introduction for 2019 AFL-CIO MLK Drum Major for Justice Award.* Retrieved by https://www.youtube.com/watch?v=eQ1OEZb8UfY

[104] Portside. (2019). *Flight Attendants President Calls for General Strike to End Government Shutdown - The Fierce Urgency of Now.* Retrieved by https://portside.org/2019-01-24/flight-attendants-president-calls-general-strike-end-government-shutdown-fierce-urgency

[105] U.S. Bureau of Labor Statistics. (2021). *Economic News Release – Union Members Summary.* Retrieved by https://www.bls.gov/news.release/union2.nr0.htm

[106] Economic Policy Institute. (2012). *Union decline and rising inequality in two charts.* Retrieved by https://www.epi.org/blog/union-decline-rising-inequality-charts/

[107] The Washington Post. (2018). *U.S. life expectancy declines again, a dismal trend not seen since World War I.* Retrieved by https://www.washingtonpost.com/national/health-science/us-life-expectancy-declines-again-a-dismal-trend-not-seen-since-world-war-i/2018/11/28/ae58bc8c-f28c-11e8-bc79-68604ed88993_story.html

[108] Insider NJ. (2019). *The Flow and Ebb of Liberty–NJ's Lost History of Voting Rights.* Retrieved by https://www.insidernj.com/flow-ebb-liberty-njs-lost-history/

[109] Alice Paul Institute. (n.d.). *Who Was Alice Paul?* Retrieved by https://www.alicepaul.org/about-alice-paul/

[110] Alice Paul Institute. (n.d.). Retrieved by https://www.alicepaul.org/

[111] The Washington Post. (2018). *4.4 million 2012 Obama voters stayed home in 2016 — more than a third of them black.* Retrieved by https://www.washingtonpost.com/news/politics/wp/2018/03/12/4-4-million-2012-obama-voters-stayed-home-in-2016-more-than-a-third-of-them-black/

[112] North Carolina State University, College of Agriculture and Life Sciences (2018). *Impact of Minimum Wages on the U.S. Agricultural Sector.* Retrieved by https://cals.ncsu.edu/news/the-impact-of-minimum-wages-on-the-u-s-agricultural-sector/

[113] CBS News. (2016). *America's foreclosure crisis isn't over.* Retrieved by https://www.cbsnews.com/news/americas-foreclosure-crisis-isnt-over/

[114] Economic Policy Institute. (2021). *Why the U.S. needs a $15 minimum wage.* Retrieved by https://www.epi.org/publication/why-america-needs-a-15-minimum-wage/

[115] CBS News. (2016). *Undocumented own U.S. homes, pay billions in taxes.* Retrieved by https://www.cbsnews.com/news/undocumented-own-u-s-homes-and-pay-billions-in-taxes/

[116] History. (2009). *A. Philip Randolph.* Retrieved by https://www.history.com/topics/black-history/a-philip-randolph

[117] New York Daily News. (2015). *SOUTH BRONX SIZZLE: Once a symbol of urban blight, the formerly burned out neighborhood is now a major draw for investors.* Retrieved by https://www.nydailynews.com/life-style/real-estate/south-bronx-real-estate-market-suddenly-burning-hot-article-1.2178095

[118] Nancy Foner. *One Out of Three: Immigrant New York in the Twenty-First Century.* (Columbia University Press, 2013).

[119] NYC.gov. (n.d.). *IDNYC.* Retrieved by https://www1.nyc.gov/site/idnyc/index.page

[120] New York Daily News. (2021). *Daily News workers vote to join NewsGuild of New York.* Retrieved by https://www.nydailynews.com/new-york/ny-new-york-daily-news-union-vote-20210430-xpnxvpvkcncyxnrd57tm2df7sy-story.html

[121] New York Daily News. (2021) *Please buy this newspaper: A Daily News reporter begs a local owner to rescue the tabloid from Alden Global Capital.* Retrieved by https://www.nydailynews.com/opinion/ny-oped-please-buy-this-newspaper-20210505-nsimwwkfczdzth3uqdmfozg6ay-story.html?outputType=amp

[122] The New York Times. (2021). *New York Times tech workers form a union.* Retrieved by https://www.nytimes.com/2021/04/13/business/media/new-york-times-tech-workers-form-a-union.html

[123] Economic Policy Institute. (2018). *America's slow-motion wage crisis.* Retrieved by https://www.epi.org/publication/americas-slow-motion-wage-crisis-four-decades-of-slow-and-unequal-growth-2/

[124] The New York Times. (2019). *Gannett, Now Largest U.S. Newspaper Chain, Targets 'Inefficiencies'.* Retrieved by https://www.nytimes.com/2019/11/19/business/media/gannett-gatehouse-merger.html

[125] Poynter. (2019). *Gannett lays off journalists across the country.* Retrieved by https://www.poynter.org/business-work/2019/gannett-lays-off-journalists-across-the-country/

126 The NewsGuild-CWA. (n.d.). *History*. Retrieved by https://newsguild.org/history/

127 Pew Research Center. (2020). *U.S. newspapers have shed half of their newsroom employees since 2008*. Retrieved by https://www.pewresearch.org/fact-tank/2020/04/20/u-s-newsroom-employment-has-dropped-by-a-quarter-since-2008/

128 Pew Research Center. (2019). *Newspapers Fact Sheet*. Retrieved by https://www.journalism.org/fact-sheet/newspapers/

129 Pew Research Center. (2019). *Audio and Podcasting Fact Sheet*. Retrieved by https://www.journalism.org/fact-sheet/audio-and-podcasting/

130 Pew Research Center. (2019). *Local TV News Fact Sheet*. Retrieved by https://www.journalism.org/fact-sheet/local-tv-news/

131 Pew Research Center. (2019). *Cable News Fact Sheet*. Retrieved by https://www.journalism.org/fact-sheet/cable-news/

132 Pew Research Center. (2019). *State of the News Media Methodology*. Retrieved by https://www.journalism.org/2019/07/23/state-of-the-news-media-methodology/

133 Pew Research Center. (2019). *Digital News Fact Sheet*. Retrieved by https://www.journalism.org/fact-sheet/digital-news/

134 Center for Information, Technology, and Public Life. (2020). *Addressing the decline of local news, rise of platforms, and spread of mis- and disinformation online*. Retrieved by https://citap.unc.edu/local-news-platforms-mis-disinformation/#executive-summary

135 Bureau of Labor Statistics. (2021). *Union Members – 2020. News Release*. Retrieved by https://www.bls.gov/news.release/pdf/union2.pdf

136 NPR. (2014). *Safety Changes Are Small Comfort When Oil Trains Pass*. Retrieved by https://www.npr.org/2014/07/04/328216488/safety-changes-are-small-comfort-when-oil-trains-pass

137 Bloomberg. (2012). *Reduced Tanker Rates Raise Safety Concerns, Industry Group Says*. Retrieved by https://www.bloomberg.com/news/articles/2012-04-02/reduced-tanker-rates-raise-safety-concerns-industry-group-says

138 The New York Times. (2021). *High Staff Turnover at U.S. Nursing Homes Poses Risks for Residents' Care*. Retrieved by https://www.nytimes.com/2021/03/01/health/covid-nursing-homes-staff-turnover.html

139 Forbes. (2020). *Top 1% Of U.S. Households Hold 15 Times More Wealth Than Bottom 50% Combined*. Retrieved by https://www.forbes.com/sites/tommybeer/2020/10/08/top-1-of-us-households-hold-15-times-more-wealth-than-bottom-50-combined/?sh=38ab9dab5179

[140] CBS News. (2016). *Is Delaware home to a "grand corruption"?* Retrieved by https://www.cbsnews.com/news/is-delaware-home-to-a-grand-corruption/

[141] WYNC News. (2010). *The Mayor's Money: Bloomberg Pressed on Offshore Investments.* Retrieved by https://www.wnyc.org/story/71747-the-mayors-money-bloomberg-pressed-on-offshore-investments/

[142] CBS News. (2015*). In Greece and Puerto Rico, the rot has a similar stench.* Retrieved by https://www.cbsnews.com/news/in-greece-and-puerto-rico-the-rot-has-a-similar-stench/

[143] The New York Time. (2016). *$2 Billion Worth of Free Media for Donald Trump.* Retrieved by https://www.nytimes.com/2016/03/16/upshot/measuring-donald-trumps-mammoth-advantage-in-free-media.html

[144] WBGO/Newark Public Radio. (n.d.). Retrieved by https://www.wbgo.org/#stream/0

[145] City & State New York. (2016). *Giuliani steals show at RNC with call for law and order in the wake of police deaths.* Retrieved by https://www.cityandstateny.com/articles/politics/campaigns-and-elections/giuliani.html#.WXTZmBSlcUs

[146] WhoWhatWhy. (2016). *The Media Struggles to Explain a Problem it Created.* Retrieved by https://whowhatwhy.org/culture/journalism-media/media-struggles-explain-problem-created/

[147] Barbara Ehrenreich. *Nickel And Dimed: On (Not) Getting By In America.* (Picador USA, 2011).

[148] Salon. (2016). *The talk-radio godfather of Trumpamania: What Michael Savage can tell us about America's white working class.* Retrieved by https://www.salon.com/2016/04/06/the_talk_radio_godfather_of_trumpamania_what_michael_savage_can_tell_us_about_americas_white_working_class/

[149] Salon. (2016). *A guide to the Philadelphia DNC that media won't show you, from extreme poverty to police misconduct.* Retrieved by https://www.salon.com/2016/07/13/a_guide_to_the_philadelphia_dnc_that_media_wont_show_you_from_extreme_poverty_to_police_misconduct/

[150] Salon. (2016). *GOP convention madness: Is Cleveland ready for its close-up?* Retrieved by https://www.salon.com/2016/07/03/gop_convention_madness_is_cleveland_ready_for_its_close_up/

[151] Jim Rokakis, Gus Frangos. *The Land Bank Revolution: How Ohio's Communities Fought Back Against the Foreclosure Crisis.* (Parafine Press, 2020).

[152] The Catholic Worker Movement. (n.d.). *The Catholic Worker Movement.* Retrieved by https://www.catholicworker.org/forest-history.html